NEW DIRECTIONS FOR MENTAL HEALTH SERVICES

H. Richard Lamb, *University of Southern California*
EDITOR-IN-CHIEF

Innovative Community Mental Health Programs

Leonard I. Stein
University of Wisconsin Medical School

EDITOR

Number 56, Winter 1992

JOSSEY-BASS PUBLISHERS
San Francisco

INNOVATIVE COMMUNITY MENTAL HEALTH PROGRAMS
Leonard I. Stein (ed.)
New Directions for Mental Health Services, no. 56
H. Richard Lamb, Editor-in-Chief

Microfilm copies of issues and articles are available in 16mm and 35mm, as well as microfiche in 105mm, through University Microfilms Inc., 300 North Zeeb Road, Ann Arbor, Michigan 48106.

LC 87-646993   ISSN 0193-9416   ISBN 1-55542-739-1

NEW DIRECTIONS FOR MENTAL HEALTH SERVICES is part of The Jossey-Bass Social and Behavioral Science Series and is published quarterly by Jossey-Bass Inc., Publishers, 350 Sansome Street, San Francisco, California 94104-1310 (publication number USPS 493-910). Second-class postage paid at San Francisco, California, and at additional mailing offices. POSTMASTER: Send address changes to New Directions for Mental Health, Jossey-Bass Inc., Publishers, 350 Sansome Street, San Francisco, California 94104-1310.

SUBSCRIPTIONS for 1992 cost $52.00 for individuals and $70.00 for institutions, agencies, and libraries.

EDITORIAL CORRESPONDENCE should be sent to the Editor-in-Chief, H. Richard Lamb, Department of Psychiatry and the Behavioral Sciences, U.S.C. School of Medicine, 1934 Hospital Place, Los Angeles, California 90033.

Cover photograph by Wernher Krutein/PHOTOVAULT © 1990.

 The paper used in this journal is acid-free and meets the strictest guidelines in the United States for recycled paper (50 percent recycled waste, including 10 percent post-consumer waste). Manufactured in the United States of America.

10% POST CONSUMER WASTE

CONTENTS

EDITOR'S NOTES

The deinstitutionalization movement—that is, the outplacing of patients from state hospitals to the community—largely took place between 1965 and 1975, when the state hospital population was reduced from approximately 550,000 to 120,000 patients. It was hoped that treatment with medication and living arrangements provided by family or board-and-care homes would be sufficient to keep patients stable and provide them with a decent quality of life. That goal was not achieved. Instead, patients experienced frequent relapse and a high readmission rate back to hospitals, transinstitutionalization into nursing homes, and neglect in the community—with the result that patients have drifted into the criminal justice system and homelessness.

These unexpected, unfavorable consequences were largely a product of our ignorance. In essence, we simply did not know that patients in the community would require a wide variety of supports—housing, financial, social, and so on. And just as important, we did not know that these supports would have to be delivered by specialized interventions that were themselves unknown. We are still in the process of developing those interventions.

To spur the development of the necessary technology, the Robert Wood Johnson Foundation created the Mental Health Services Development Program. Initiated in 1987, the project supported eighteen state and local initiatives designed to improve access to a broad range of health care and community services for the chronically mentally ill. This volume reports on six of those projects.

New technology requires people to change their mode of practice—rarely an easy thing to do. The first chapter in this volume—by Leonard I. Stein—is a case study of the change process in the development by Stein and Test of the Training in Community Living Program in Madison, Wisconsin. It describes the barriers to change and the strategies used to overcome them.

The six remaining chapters fall into two groups: three chapters that address innovation in organization of services, and three that describe innovative services for special populations.

Vocational rehabilitation for the mentally ill has been moving away from prevocational training to in vivo training in competitive employment sites. Getting persons into jobs has proven to be much easier than expected—having those persons stay employed has been a problem. In Chapter Two, Judith A. Cook and Lisa Razzano describe an innovative program developed at Thresholds in Chicago to help promote long-term job retention.

Thankfully, the debate over community-based versus hospital-based treatment is over. The most productive dialogue now concerns the most useful role each can play in helping persons with serious and persistent mental illness achieve a stable life of decent quality. In Chapter Three, Carl A. Cappello, Howard D. Reid, and John H. Simsarian describe how a state hospital, reconceptualizing itself as not bounded by walls, has developed a full array of services, both hospital and community, in a previously underserved area of the state. Their work can serve as a model for how state hospitals can become an integral and vital part of a well-functioning system of care.

The consumer movement to provide peer support is an exciting development in mental health services. In Chapter Four, Lawrence Telles describes an innovative project in Santa Clara, California, that extends the concept further. He sketches the development of a client community built around housing. In this community, the role of the professional staff is to tend to the community, not the individual client. Thus, staff act more like community organizers than clinicians, and community members provide support and help to each other.

As if mental illness and substance abuse are not enough of a challenge, try adding problems with the law to that mix. That is exactly what Rhode Island did. In Chapter Five, Ann Detrick and Virginia Stiepock describe a program developed in Rhode Island to serve this triply burdened population. The program is showing very encouraging results.

The size of the aging population is growing dramatically and will continue to do so for some time. There is, however, comparatively little in the literature regarding treatment of the older person with serious and persistent mental illness. Senior Health and Peer Counseling of Santa Monica, California, has been a leader in developing innovative health services for older persons. In Chapter Six, Marla Hassinger Martin and Bernice Bratter describe how their agency addressed the needs of older adults with serious mental illness living in their community.

The first chapter was a personal account of bringing about a change in services. The last chapter in this volume is a personal account of an innovative program to help the homeless mentally ill living on the streets of Skid Row in Los Angeles. Picture a person dressed virtually in rags, with long hair meeting a beard, so that only the eyes can be seen—know that this person has avoided human contact for years—and you will have some idea of the challenge faced by those who want to gain the trust and participation in treatment of the homeless mentally ill. Mollie Lowery tells the story of LAMP, a program dedicated to the homeless mentally ill. It is not only a story of what needs to be done and how to do it; it is a story of personal commitment. For those of us in the helping professions, Lowery's story is an important reminder that the most important healing instrument we have is our caring, commitment, and humanity.

As editor of this volume, I want to think the Robert Wood Johnson Foundation for its commitment to investing in programs designed to help the least fortunate among us. I also want to thank and congratulate the recipients of the Robert Wood Johnson Foundation's Mental Health Services Development Program for their creativity and hard work in developing successful programs that can serve as models for others to emulate.

Leonard I. Stein
Editor

LEONARD I. STEIN is professor of psychiatry at the University of Wisconsin Medical School, Madison, Wisconsin, and director of research and education at the Mental Health Center of Dane County, Madison, Wisconsin.

The change process is rarely easy; it is especially difficult when it requires people to alter their professional practices significantly.

Innovating Against the Current

Leonard I. Stein

Innovation starts with an idea. What happens to the idea once it is exposed to public scrutiny is greatly influenced by the environment surrounding it. If the idea is congruent with the traditions, philosophy, and practice of the environment in which it was spawned, it will be nurtured, protected, and encouraged to grow and bear fruit. If, on the other hand, the idea is contrary to, or inconsistent with, the traditions of its environment its life is much more hazardous, its rate of growth is slower, and its chances of growing strong enough to bear fruit are reduced. This chapter is the story of such an idea—an idea originating in an environment that was eager to encourage innovation but that was reluctant to permit the development of an innovation that was contrary to its major mode of practice.

Influence of the Environment on Innovation

Innovation is a product, and activities to produce it are expected in organizations that identify that product as one of its goals. Thus, we expect innovation from universities and from the research and development sections of industrial corporations. We do not normally expect it from organizations whose primary—and often only—responsibility is to provide service. In the early 1960s, Mendota State Hospital in Madison, Wisconsin, was a state mental hospital in the business of serving patients by providing them clinical treatment and serving society by protecting it from dangerous patients. Not unlike many of the progressive state hospitals around the country, it had a good staff, a large patient population, and both a high preadmission and a high discharge rate. In addition, it had a small office of research and education staffed by a single individual.

In the mid 1960s, two events occurred that greatly modified the character of the institution. First, the hospital made a major decision to

NEW DIRECTIONS FOR MENTAL HEALTH SERVICES, no. 56, Winter 1992 © Jossey-Bass Publishers increase its research activities and enlarge its research department. Thus, in a real sense it declared that, in addition to service, the hospital was now seriously in the business of producing innovation. Second, the hospital hired an innovative new director of research and education. The new director, Arnold Ludwig, was an energetic, skillful administrator who was successful in getting the hospital to dedicate an entire ward with a full complement of staff to research activities. He formed a special treatment unit (STU), a research unit whose primary goal was the development of new *inpatient* treatment techniques for persons with chronic schizophrenia. In addition to the usual ward staff, he attracted two young and talented clinician/researchers, Arnold Marx, a psychiatrist, and Mary Ann Test, a psychologist, to work with him. Together they designed and implemented a variety of novel psychosocial treatment techniques within a research design context.

Although there were some minor struggles regarding some of the treatment approaches with staff in other units, and occasionally with the administration, the overall atmosphere in the institution was to support the research on the STU. The administration was particularly supportive of the STU research and ran interference for that unit when other staff in the hospital raised questions or objections to the research program. This was not surprising, since the institution had by then identified itself as providing innovation as a major goal, along with service. And importantly, the innovation was consistent with the traditions, philosophy, and operation of the hospital. The innovations were carried out in an inpatient setting; the roles of the various professional and paraprofessional groups working on the STU were the same as those on the service units. In essence, the innovations were going with the current, and thus received the support of the institution.

A Change in Focus: Going Against the Current

Through the programs of the STU, Ludwig, Marx, and Test demonstrated that a variety of novel psychosocial treatment techniques could have an impact on previously unresponsive patients and could significantly enhance their *in-hospital* functioning. Even when treatment approaches were unsuccessful, they were important learning experiences that led Ludwig, Marx, and Text to consider alternative treatment techniques. The format and outcome of these treatment research programs, as well as process data and theoretical implications, were carefully documented (Ludwig, 1968).

While the major emphasis of the projects was on inpatient treatment, we also gained experience and expertise that would be helpful in providing patients with community care after discharge from STU. However, it was not an uncommon experience for patients who were discharged in a stable condition to be readmitted to the hospital, once again psychotic, in a relatively short time. This revolving-door phenomenon was happening not only on the STU, but also on the acute service units of the hospital, reflecting a national trend.

When Ludwig left in 1970 to become chairman of the department of psychiatry of the University of Kentucky Medical School, I took over his position as director of research and education, and Marx and Test assumed the leadership of the STU. These changes in leadership made possible a marked shift in the direction that future STU programs would take. Ludwig had been primarily interested in learning more about using psychosocial techniques in an inpatient setting, whereas Marx, Test, and I were interested in helping patients sustain their community tenure. It became increasingly clear to us that the crucial variable in producing success after discharge was an intensive and sustained program of supports and treatment in the community. We decided to change the focus of research from activities in an *inpatient* setting designed to prepare patients to live in the community, to activities in an *outpatient* setting designed to help patients make a sustained adjustment to community life. We obtained a small grant to do a pilot study termed "The Prevention of Institutionalization Program," which resulted in a paper by Marx, Test, and Stein entitled "Extro-Hospital Management of Severe Mental Illness" (1973). Following the pilot project, Test and I wrote a sizable NIMH grant, which led to our studies of community treatment of persons with mental illness.

I will describe these studies in detail later in the chapter, but first I want to discuss the immediate changes in staff functions that occurred in both the pilot study and the larger study that followed. Staff would no longer report to the hospital and work on an inpatient ward. Instead they would report to work at an old house in downtown Madison, Wisconsin, where they would spend approximately forty-five minutes to an hour making plans for how they would work with patients in vivo in the community. For the rest of the time, most of the staff, particularly nurses and aides, would work with patients in their homes, neighborhoods, places of work, and places of recreation. Only the nurses carried beepers and could be contacted at any time; the aides would be out of contact for hours at a time. In short, from the hospital's point of view, this innovation differed from prior research in that its operations were not congruent with the customary traditions, philosophy, and practice of the hospital. Thus, rather than going with the current, it was going against the current. This resulted in a change in how the hospital administration related to the research enterprise. Instead of supporting and nurturing the research effort as it did when the research was carried out in an inpatient setting, the administration was now throwing up barriers. Some examples of the administration's concerns follow.

Justification for Training Time

The staff would now be involved in a very different kind of activity. Rather than traditional inpatient work, which is well defined and circumscribed, the staff would be working in an open system. They would be working with patients in the community who did not have to do what they were told; they would have to negotiate with landlords, take care of the complaints of shopkeepers, and work collaboratively with the police and with a whole host of agencies from various levels of government. It was clear to us that the staff would need to be free of their clinical responsibilities for a period of time in order to be trained. The administration had a problem with this: "How can we justify all that staff time with no service being provided?"

Transportation and Liability

The staff would need to be mobile and do quite a bit of traveling around town. Customarily, when the hospital needed to transport patients, it used the state cars it had available; however, the state was certainly not going to provide state cars to all of our staff. We understood this and negotiated with the staff about using their own cars. Administrators were concerned that not enough money had been budgeted for reimbursement of travel expenses, and that liability issues would not allow staff to transport patients in their own cars.

Who Will Be Watching the Aides? As noted above, the staff would be spending their time moving around the community, and the aides would be out of contact for hours at a time. The administration was thus concerned that the aides might not be working when out of contact. "What's to stop them from going to a movie or going home for a period of time?" they wondered.

Can You Eat Lunch and Not Have It Count as Your Lunch Hour? At times, the staff would be involved in teaching patients how to use the local inexpensive restaurants. It would be quite awkward for a staff person teaching the patient how to order lunch not to eat along with the patient. We decided that since the staff was actually working during that lunchtime, that period would not be considered a lunch break. The administration raised an objection, asking how the staff could eat lunch without counting that as a lunch break: "Isn't that giving the staff two lunch breaks?"

The administration was in a bind. The hospital had developed a reputation, through Ludwig and his colleagues, as an organization that, in addition to providing service, had an important product—research— to produce. The administration had actively publicized that fact. Now their innovators wanted to do something that was making them uncomfortable. Their innovators wanted to behave in ways that were not consistent with the traditions, philosophy, and operation of the institution. The administration attempted to deal with this bind by putting up enough barriers to influence the innovators to choose an innovation that would be more consistent with the institution. However, Stein, Test, and Marx were convinced that they were onto something important and were iconoclastic enough to be spurred forward by the barriers rather than succumbing to them.

Administrators were ambivalent. They wanted research, but not the kind their researchers wanted to do. The researchers, on the other hand, were not at all ambivalent. They wanted to do research and were committed to doing the research they had in mind. Through the researchers' persistence, negotiation efforts, and goodwill, the administration finally okayed a period of time for staff training, and allocated money for the needed transportation. The administration was reassured that the liability issue could be managed by the insurers of the staff's cars and that staff would be sufficiently supervised. Also, it finally yielded to the notion that a staff person eating lunch while training a patient should not need to count this as a lunch break.

Description of the Training in Community Living (TCL) Program

In brief, the program was implemented by mental hospital ward staff who were transplanted to the community. Staff coverage was available twenty-four hours a day, seven days a week. Patient programs were individually tailored and were based primarily on an assessment of the patient's coping-skill deficits and requirements for community living. Most treatment took place in vivo: in patients' homes, neighborhoods, and places of work. More specifically, staff members on the scene in patients' homes and neighborhoods taught and assisted them in daily living activities such as laundry upkeep, shopping, cooking, restaurant use, grooming, budgeting, and use of transportation. In addition, patients were given sustained and intensive assistance in finding a job or sheltered workshop placement, and the staff then continued their daily contact with patients and patients' supervisors or employers to help resolve on-the-job problems. Staff guided patients in the constructive use of leisure time, and in the development of effective social skills. In fact, they prodded and supported patients to involve themselves in recreational and social activities. They capitalized on patients' strengths rather than focusing on their pathology. Also, providing support to patients, patients' families, and community members was a key function of the staff. The program was "assertive"; if a patient did not show up for work, a staff member immediately went to the patient's home to help with any problem that was interfering. Each patient's medical status was carefully monitored and treated; medication was routinely used for schizo-phrenic and manic-depressive patients (Stein and Test, 1980).

Anticipating Barriers to Dissemination

Dissemination of new psychosocial approaches to the care of persons with severe and persistent mental illness has an uneven history. Unfortu-nately, we do not know the detailed history of the dissemination of moral treatment in hospitals, but we do know that it spread rapidly from the York Retreat in England to the colonies in America. A much more recent and highly successful (in terms of dissemination) program was the spread of the therapeutic community and milieu treatment. It was not long after Scotland's Maxwell Jones described the therapeutic community that it swept through the hospitals in the United States. There is a question as to whether Jones would certify all those therapeutic communities as fulfill-ing his requirements; however, there is no question that at least in name, state hospitals, as well as private hospitals throughout the country, developed programs at least resembling the therapeutic· community al-most overnight. Although in Jones's therapeutic community the roles of staff vis-à-vis one another and the power differential between staff and patients changed, that was rarely the case in the "therapeutic communi-ties" spreading throughout our state hospitals in the United States. Thus, the therapeutic community movement in practice remained consistent with the traditions, philosophy, and operation of the mental hospital, and it was therefore nurtured by them. On the other hand, George Fairweather had a difficult time getting his lodge program dissemi-nated—largely, in my judgment, because it ran against the current and significantly changed the day-to-day functioning of staff as well as the power differential between patients and staff.

We, the innovators of the TCL program, recognized that we would have a difficult time disseminating our program, and thus we gave considerable thought to the barriers that would need to be overcome for dissemination to have a chance.

A Tight Research Design

We were aware that a simple description of the program, with anec-dotes of its success, would be easily discounted. Thus, a tight research design was necessary. An experiment was designed to study the effects on patient functioning during their intensive community treatment in the TCL and to evaluate patients' functioning afterward when they were transferred to traditional community programs. To accomplish this, the TCL model was rigorously evaluated by comparing it with a control group that received progressive in-hospital treatment plus the usual kinds of community aftercare available at that time. Subjects were assigned to the TCL approach for fourteen months, after which they received no further input from the experimental unit staff. The last few months of the fourteen-month period were used to gradually wean the patients, integrating them into existing programs that were essentially the same programs that treated the control group.

All patients seeking admission to the state hospital for inpatient care were screened to see if they met the following three criteria: (1) They had to be residents of Dane County, Wisconsin (Madison and the surrounding area—the county in which the hospital was located). (2) They were required to be between the ages of eighteen and sixty-two years. (3) They could have *any* diagnosis other than severe organic brain syndrome or primary alcoholism. Patients meeting these criteria became subjects of the study and were randomly assigned to the experimental or control group by the admission office staff. Control subjects were treated in the hospital for as long as necessary and then were linked with appropriate community agencies. Experimental subjects did not enter the hospital, except in rare instances, but instead received the TCL approach for fourteen months before integration into existing community programs. Assessment data on all patients were gathered at the baseline (time of admission into the study) and every four months, for twenty-eight months, through face-to-face interviews by a research staff that operated independently of both clinical teams. Data on experimental subjects who were hospitalized were reported. *No* patients were excluded on the basis of severity of symptomatology or for any reason other than failure to meet the three specific admission criteria.

A variety of assessment instruments were used, including a form collecting standard demographic data on life situation and economic variables, a measure of symptomatology, and a measure of community adjustment that recorded the patient's living situation, time spent in institutions, employment record, leisure-time activities, social relationships, quality of environment, and subjective satisfaction with life.

Cost

We were hopeful that our results would show a significant benefit for patients in terms of their tenure in the community and their functioning while in the community. However, we correctly anticipated that we would be questioned about the relative cost of this treatment. I say "correctly anticipated" because the scenario that we envisioned indeed happened over and over again. We would present our findings showing a positive clinical outcome; inevitably, among the first questions asked after the presentation would be the following: "It all sounds well and good, but aren't the costs prohibitive?" We needed to know the answer to that question. Fortunately, a close friend of mine, Burton Weisbrod, was an economist with a national reputation for his work in health economics. Burt and I were in the habit of sailing my boat every Sunday morning, and he was getting "hooked" on sailing and was appreciative of the opportunity to sail with me. I unashamedly took advantage of that situation and pressed him to cooperate with us in heading up a team to do a benefit-cost study of the TCL model as compared to traditional treatments. I had envisioned it as an "accounting" job, and was delighted when he turned it into a sophisticated study that took into consideration not only monetary factors, but factors that could not be monetized. I believe this study still stands today as a model for studies of this nature (Weisbrod, Test, and Stein, 1980).

Family and Community Burden

Deinstitutionalization was in full swing. Tens of thousands of patients were being discharged into communities unprepared for their care. In fact, they could not be prepared, because in a real sense we did not know what they needed. We made the incorrect assumption that all the patient would need would be periodic visits to the mental health center to get his or her medication evaluated and represcribed. As a consequence of this inadequate care, patients were having a difficult time in the community, relapsing into psychosis and requiring frequent readmissions, being neglected, and ending up homeless or in jail. In fact, our TCL program was designed to address these problems. However, it was not only the patients that were suffering, but also family and community members. Much concern was being expressed over the possible burden being placed on family and community members by programs that emphasized community treatment of severely disturbed patients. This was being reflected in the literature, which revealed a fear that though deinstitutionalization might be helpful to patients, it could cause considerable psychological and social disturbance among community members coming in contact with them. That could likely be another barrier to dissemination. We pictured another scenario. If, as we had anticipated, our research showed a positive clinical outcome, and if a benefit-cost study demonstrated that the program would not be economically prohibitive, we could imagine someone saying, in a question-and-answer period, "It sounds fine for the patients, and the costs seem okay, but what about the burden you're imposing on family and community members?" Thus, we also did a concurrent third study, which was to measure the social costs of our TCL program as compared with the traditional approach of using short-term hospitalization plus aftercare. Six objective and one subjective measures of the burden placed on the family members of patients in both groups were obtained.

Community burden was also assessed through police records of frequency of patient arrests, number of suicidal gestures that required medical attention, and frequency of emergency room use (Test and Stein, 1980).

The Period of Jeopardy—One Tragedy and It Is All Over!

The subjects for our study were patients coming to the state hospital for admission. This is the last stop for patients; we received patients brought in, handcuffed, by police; patients transferred from psychiatric units of general hospitals because they could not be "managed on that unit"; patients committed by a judge for treatment in a hospital (we had an agreement with the judge that if a patient was randomly assigned to our study, we could walk the patient out of the hospital and treat him or her in the community); and patients brought in by family members with a letter signed by a physician that the patient *required* hospital treatment. We of course tried to use good clinical judgment and to hospitalize anyone we thought was imminently suicidal or homicidal (those hospital days would show up in our results as charged against experimental patients), but we were interested in pushing the limits and trying to find out if we could treat virtually all potential admissions who were not suicidal or homicidal. Thus it was necessary for the vast majority of patients to be treated in the community rather than being admitted to the hospital. We had to do a balancing act: if we were too cautious, the experiment would lose a great deal of meaning and impact, but if we were not cautious enough, serious harm could be done.

As it turned out, we only hospitalized twelve of sixty-five patients for a mean of eleven days per patient; thus, a great many highly symptomatic patients were not admitted but were treated in the community. However, the program was in constant jeopardy. If within the first few months, we had one tragedy—a suicide, a homicide, a rape, or some other behavior that would bring our program notoriously to the public's attention—I truly believe now, as we believed then, that it would have been all over for us. One tragedy, and I would get a call from the hospital superintendent telling us to close up shop and come home. This is rarely true of innovations that do not run contrary to the current. I recently saw a documentary on renal transplantation; early in the game, the mortality rate was extremely high in terms of the short amount of time patients lived following the transplant. However, no one stopped that program, even though dialysis had been perfected sufficiently to keep patients alive for long periods of time. Running against the current is a hazardous business, and we were extremely fortunate in not having a tragedy that would have prematurely shortened the life of our program.

Results of the Experiments

In brief, the results of our experiments are as follows:

Clinical Evaluation

The research was designed to have two phases of clinical intervention for the experimental group. The first phase was twelve months of intensive involvement in TCL, followed by two months of weaning the patient onto the existing system; in the second fourteen-month phase, experimental patients received, in essence, the same clinical intervention as controls. The results of the first fourteen months showed a striking advantage for experimental patients over control patients. Of the sixty-five patients in the control group, fifty-seven were hospitalized for a mean of thirty-six days per patient. In addition, the control patients experienced a 60 percent readmission rate, which was approximately what they had been experiencing prior to coming into the study, and which is the common percentage of the readmissions reported nationally by public mental hospitals. In the experimental group, on the other hand, only twelve of sixty-five patients were hospitalized, for a mean of eleven days. Importantly, the revolving door was virtually eliminated, with a readmission rate under 10 percent.

Other significant differences favoring the experimental group over the control group are as follows: symptomatology, employment, social relationships, and, very important, a subjective satisfaction with life. On no measure did the control group do better than the experimental group.

In the second fourteen-month period, when the experimental group was being treated with conventional treatment, the gains made during the first period began to deteriorate. There was a gradual, but definite, increase in hospital use by the experimental group, whereas the control group remained stable. Likewise, the improved social relationships decreased, subjective satisfaction with life decreased, symptomatology increased, and time spent in sheltered employment began to decline strikingly. The only gain made by the experimental group in the first phase that did not deteriorate was money earned in competitive employment.

At first blush, this deterioration in the second phase was a disappointment. However, on further consideration, I believe this was the most important finding of the study. Specifically, it clearly demonstrated that the strategies we had been using in mental health to date were failing these patients. We were using time-limited strategies: day treatment programs were set up for six months or one year, after which time the patient was supposed no longer to need them; supportive psychotherapy was set up for a specific period; after which patients were no longer to need it; living situations were structured so that they were transitional in nature, whereby it was expected that after a specified period, the patient would have to move on to permanent living situations. All of these strategies were based on a "cure" or "preparation" model. What this experiment made clear was that we needed to shift from a time-limited model to a model that provided services indefinitely. In retrospect, it seems obvious that when we deal with an illness that we do not know how to prevent or cure—and that is thus chronic in nature—the intervention likewise must be long term in nature.

Another important finding of the study was that patients needed help making a sustained and satisfactory life in the community. Thus, treatment programs needed to expand their interest from just psychological interventions to interventions that addressed such everyday problems as material resources (food, shelter, clothing, and medical care). And staff needed to add some of the following to their repertoire of "helping" functions: teaching coping skills to meet the demands of community life; providing enough support to keep the patient motivated to persevere and remain involved with life; helping families and patients work through their problems, utilizing a problem-solving approach rather than a psychotherapeutic approach; and supporting and educating community members who were involved with patients—such as law enforcement personnel, agency people, landlords, shopkeepers, and so on—to help them relate in a manner both beneficial to the patients and acceptable to the community members. Finally, these interventions needed to be carried out by a team of workers that *assertively* worked in vivo when necessary, helping patients and the community with the above.

Economic Benefit-Cost Analysis

A benefit-cost analysis should be seen not as a mechanism for deciding mechanically on the allocation of funds and resources among programs, but as a structure for weighing advantages and disadvantages (that is, for organizing knowledge). Considering all the forms of benefits and costs that were derived in monetary terms, the experimental program provided both additional benefits and additional costs as compared with conventional treatment. However, the added benefits— some $1,200 per patient per year—are nearly $400 more per patient per year than the added costs. Also, a number of the benefits and costs measured in quantitative but nonmonetary terms showed additional advantages of the community-based experimental program (decrease of symptomatology, increased satisfaction with life, and so on). The bottom line of the economic study was that the differences in costs between the experimental program and the control program were small, whereas the benefits, especially the clinical benefits, were dramatically better.

Social Costs

As noted earlier, much concern has been raised over the possible burden placed on family and community members by programs that emphasize community treatment of severely disturbed patients. In sum, all measures showed that the total in-community program resulted in no more burden on the family or community than the traditional approach. The large amount of support provided to patients, families, and community members in the experimental approach was probably responsible for there being no increase in burden despite the fact that severely disturbed patients were treated in the community.

Consequences of the Innovation

I believe the major consequence of this innovation in the treatment arena was to change how we think about treating persons with severe and persistent mental illness. The principles of having no arbitrary time limits for programs and broadening mental health intervention to include helping patients with housing, finances, shopping, food preparation, laundry, and so on are now well accepted. It is also now well accepted that treatment is not facility-bound, whether that facility be a hospital or a mental health center, and that staff must work in the field with the patient. When we first advocated those principles, we met a great deal of resistance, couched primarily in terms suggesting that those functions are not mental health functions. There have also been consequences for patients, staff, and the community.

Patients. Consequences for patients must be seen in context. Virtually all communities in the United States now say they are providing community support services. However, where those services do not follow the principles outlined in this chapter or where they are so inadequately provided as to have little impact on patients, the negative consequences of high relapse rates with high readmissions, homelessness, and a drift into the criminal justice system occur. Several studies have shown that where a good system of care following these principles is provided, on the other hand, the consequences for patients have been very beneficial (Stein, 1987).

Over the past fifteen years, I have seen an interesting shift in how patients have learned to cope with stress. When the primary mode of treatment for persons with severe and persistent mental illness was the hospital, patients learned to use the hospital as a major coping mechanism. Thus, if they experienced stress, they would often appear in the emergency room requesting hospitalization. Working with patients who use this coping mechanism is very different from working with patients who have learned to take advantage of the supportive system available to them in the community. Specifically, it has taken a great deal of effort to keep that earlier group of patients out of the hospital long enough—and to see them through enough episodes of stress—for them to learn to use the community system. We have a much easier time with the group of patients who have never learned to use the hospital as a coping mechanism.

Staff. In 1975, I left the experimental program to take a position in the county mental health center to attempt to influence the system of care in Dane County, Wisconsin, to adopt many of the methods we developed in our experimental program. Fortunately, the administrators of the mental health center, as well as leaders in the county mental health board, were interested in seeing these changes take place. Specifically, they wanted the mental health system to put more of resources into treating persons with severe illness and fewer into psychotherapy treatment for persons with less severe illness.

Like most of this country's mental health centers in the mid 1970s, this center was primarily a large outpatient psychotherapy clinic, operating from 9:00 to 5:00 Monday through Friday, providing psychotherapy to patients with nonpsychotic diagnoses and offering little to patients with psychotic diagnoses. The staff of the mental health center was understandably resistant to change. They had gone into the field to be psychotherapists, they were trained as psychotherapists in their professional schools, and their major role models—their professors—were primarily psychotherapists. Thus, it was not surprising that when staff providing psychotherapy were asked to do something quite different, they would resist change. In fact, only a small number of staff actually changed their *mode* of functioning; the major change was *where* they functioned. When they were given the forced choice of either leaving the mental health center or working in one of these new programs, most only worked in the new programs until they could find another job where they could do psychotherapy (many went into private practice). New workers who were hired specifically to do this job (many from the hospital setting) had little difficulty doing it and liking what they were doing.

Community. The effect on the community was very interesting. Since we provided a great deal of support to patients and to their families, we received a lot of support from families in return. Landlords, on the whole, were not unhappy with having a large number of chronic mentally ill people living in the community, since it increased the number of available renters. They were provided with a staff that was available to the landlord approximately twenty-four hours a day if problems arise, but even more important, the staff ensured that the rent was paid in a timely fashion. The business community, on the whole, was unhappy with the situation. They had people who appeared eccentric coming to their stores and often spending a lot of time there. The staff was always available to shopkeepers, but what the shopkeepers really wanted was for the staff to keep patients out of their stores. We of course did not do that, but would instead give them tactful civic lectures about the necessity for tolerating deviant behavior as long as that deviant behavior was not law-breaking. We worked closely with them, modeling for them how they should relate to our patients.

We had several episodes where we had to threaten to go to court if our patients' civil rights were not honored. For example, the local YMCA was often used to house patients for short periods of time until we could find permanent housing for them. Local businessmen, who used the YMCA during the day for their exercise workouts, began to complain about the other clientele they would run into in the lobby. The board of directors of the YMCA met and attempted to resolve the problem by making a rule that anyone with a psychiatric history could not utilize YMCA housing. We met with the board and needed to threaten a court action if they did not rescind that policy. They eventually rescinded it and in fact became active in providing support to our patients, not only by supporting them in the YMCA lobby but by starting a patient club in the community as well.

Not all stories end so happily. Like most downtown businesses without sufficient parking to compete with suburban shopping centers, the downtown stores in Madison lost a good deal of their business. At one point, the downtown businesspeople decided the increasing visibility of chronic patients in the downtown area was the cause of this decline. There were headlines in newspapers stating this as a major problem for downtown business. In fact, a city council member attempted to pass a resolution in the City Council to have buses pick up patients and drop them off at the suburban shopping centers. The resolution of course did not pass, but it was a reflection of the kinds of feelings that people had.

Now, some years later, this is no longer an issue. The community on the whole is not happy about the situation but has come to accept the fact that many persons with severe and persistent mental illness are living among them. They are aware that mental health professionals are available around the clock to come and help when necessary, and most important, they are aware that they cannot do anything about "getting rid of these people." Indeed, the community seems to have accepted the fact that persons with chronic mental illness are now a permanent fixture. This change has taken at least a decade.

Dissemination—Swimming Against a Tidal Wave

Wide dissemination of this model would have enormous consequences for how and where mental health professionals in the public system would be operating. It would mean that the primary locus of care would shift from the hospital to the community, with a concomitant reduction in the numbers of hospitals and the numbers of the employees required to work in them. That would entail a major shift in funding—from hospitals to communities. Thus, it would have an enormous effect on the power base of the administrators in state government who would lose those funds, and on the power of employee unions that are much stronger in hospital settings than in most community settings. Staying with the imagery employed in the title of this chapter, "Innovating Against the Current," wide dissemination would be like swimming against a tidal wave.

Not surprisingly, resistance came from many quarters. Hospitals decried this movement as being harmful to patients and pointed to tragedies that had happened all over the country during the movement of deinstitutionalization. They of course neglected to point out that these tragedies were happening where there were inadequate services for patients in the community. In some states, the hospital unions have been so politically powerful as to essentially block effective dissemination of these kinds of programs. As noted earlier, mental health workers doing traditional psychotherapy in the community were also highly resistant to change.

Fortunately, certain forces were exerting pressure to develop the kinds of programs described in this chapter. State governments were feeling the economic pinch of rising hospital costs and were anxious to reduce those costs, primarily by shifting them to federal cost centers. In addition, they could legitimately buttress their argument by pointing to the effectiveness of community programs in helping this population. There have now been several replications of this work with essentially the same findings, as well as a whole host of other effective community-based interventions that help this population, ranging from housing to employment (Stein, 1987).

When those resistant to change were confronted with the successes of innovative programs such as the one described here and were asked how they could continue to resist change in light of evidence showing how much better patients were doing with a new approach, the response they gave was unanticipated and frustrating to counter. They readily admitted that the program was successful in helping patients, that it was economically feasible, and that it did not increase family or community burden. But they quickly pointed out that the program was a "model" program, and added, "We all know model programs are developed by especially energetic and creative people, and will only work if those kinds of people are running it, and further, that these programs are only specific to the area in which they were developed and have limited usefulness in terms of transportability."

What was so frustrating about trying to fight this barrier was that it was the classic "Catch 22," with the "catch" going something like this: for a program to be even considered for exportation, it must of course prove its effectiveness; if it is effective, however, it is then obviously a "model" program, and we all know that model programs have limited usefulness in terms of transportability. To support this argument, proponents of that explanation generally cited other innovations in health care, from transplant surgery to use of the CAT scan, and pointed out how quickly they had become routine procedures. They argued that the fact that community-based care for persons with severe and persistent mental illness had not developed as quickly as some of these other health procedures was proof that the program must require very energetic and creative people—and a very special, receptive environment.

I cannot tell you how many times, in the early years, I heard that argument for why programs like this could not be widely implemented. Now—a decade later—it is rare to encounter that objection, because programs like this are being developed in many areas at an accelerating rate. The argument failed to take into consideration several crucial factors that influence how quickly an innovation becomes standard practice. Kidney transplants and CAT scans were innovations that were consistent with the traditions, philosophy, and thus practice of their respective fields. Indeed, in those fields, the development of new technology is constantly sought after and quickly disseminated. These innovations do not change the basic practices of the clinicians, and, very important, do not change the hierarchy or role relationships of the key players. The new innovations are frequently made by faculty and first put into operation in teaching hospitals. Thus, they are quickly incorporated into the curriculum, and trainees are motivated to emulate their faculty role models in practicing the innovation when they leave training. Although these innovations are made by especially energetic and creative people, the practitioners of these innovations do not need to share these characteristics. Further, the innovation itself supports the established structure, and in return is supported by it. Given these conditions, it is not surprising that dissemination occurs rapidly.

Contrast that with community-based care of persons with severe and persistent mental illness. Although some of the innovators ended up in universities, almost all of the innovation was done while the innovators worked in public settings, and the model programs themselves were developed in public settings, not universities. Rather than being consistent with the traditions, philosophy, and practice of the field, the innovations were incompatible with them. A hundred years of hospital treatment, as the primary locus of care for persons with chronic mental illness, was challenged. The basic practice of clinicians changed dramatically from individual and group talking therapies in an institutional setting to an approach emphasizing community support and rehabilitation in a community setting. These new models required a change in the role relationships of the key players from a hierarchical model to a much more egalitarian one. This became necessary since so much of the hands-on work and patient contact was being done by nonmedical mental health professionals and paraprofessionals outside of medically oriented institutions. Since this innovation occurred outside of the universities, students in the professional schools were not being prepared to do this kind of work. Quite the contrary, they were still being trained to operate in the traditional system and were taught by their role models, the faculty, who themselves were practicing in the traditional way. In short, the innovation of using the community as the primary locus of care for persons with chronic mental illness was not compatible with the established structure and thus was not supported by it—in fact, it was at times actively resisted by it. Therefore, it is not at all surprising that dissemination of this innovation requires much more time to happen.

Given the above conditions, I am surprised by how rapidly the innovation has progressed, and indeed, by how much—in terms of standard practice—things have changed. In the 1970s, the notions of staff outreaching to patients in their homes and neighborhoods, supporting them in permanent supported living arrangements, and utilizing alternatives to hospitalization when relapse occurred were seen as foreign to mental health practice. These practices are now generally accepted as necessary. In the 1970s, having a team designated to provide community-based continuing care to persons who were resistant to treatment and who were chronically mentally ill was an innovation that only existed in Madison, Wisconsin. Now, Continuing Care Teams (also known as Training in Community Living Teams or as Programs of Assertive Community Treatment) are operating in many communities from coast to coast and proliferating rapidly. In the 1970s, none of the schools teaching mental health professionals were training them how to do this kind of work. Now a growing number of schools are doing so, and the American Psychiatric Association is in the process of developing a model curriculum to be used by departments of psychiatry to train their residents to do community-based work with persons with severe and persistent mental illness. There are now enough programs in operation to justify the statement that running good community treatment programs will always require competent people in the same way that doing kidney transplants requires competent surgeons. The fact is that neither requires unusually energetic or creative people.

In conclusion, when thinking about the problems inherent in innovation and dissemination, we must take two factors into account that have not received sufficient attention. First and most important, the degree to which the innovation challenges the traditions, philosophy, and thus practice of the field in which the innovation is taking place must be considered. The more an innovation runs against the current, the more obstacles it will have to overcome before being supported and disseminated. Second, when thinking about dissemination of health care models that challenge traditional practice, the time frame we adopt must be different from those we use for health care models congruent with the established structure. With innovations running against the current, we must think in terms of *decades* rather than months or years. Keeping these two factors in mind can help smooth the process of innovation.

References

Ludwig, A. M. "The Influence of Nonspecific Healing Techniques with Chronic Schizophrenics." *American Journal of Psychotherapy*, 1968, 22, 332–404.

Marx, A. J., Test, M. A., and Stein, L. I. "Extro-Hospital Management of Severe Mental Illness." *Archives of General Psychiatry*, 1973, 29, 505–511.

Stein, L. I. "Funding a System of Care for Schizophrenia." *Psychiatric Annals*, 1987, 17, 592–598.

Stein, L. I., and Test, M. A. "Alternative to Mental Hospital Treatment, I. Conceptual Model, Treatment Program, and Clinical Evaluation." *Archives of General Psychiatry*, 1980, 37, 392–397.

Test, M. A., and Stein, L. I. "Alternative to Mental Hospital Treatment, III. Social Cost." *Archives of General Psychiatry*, 1980, 37, 409–412.

Weisbrod, B., Test, M. A., and Stein, L. I. "Alternative to Mental Hospital Treatment, II. Economic Benefit-Cost Analysis." *Archives of General Psychiatry*, 1980, 37, 400–405.

LEONARD I. STEIN *is professor of psychiatry at the University of Wisconsin Medical School, Madison, Wisconsin, and director of research and education at the Mental Health Center of Dane County, Madison, Wisconsin.*

New developments in psychosocial rehabilitation have identified the need to design service delivery programs that do not simply adopt the model of supported employment used with people with developmental disabilities, but that adapt it for appropriate use for people with mental illness.

Natural Vocational Supports for Persons with Severe Mental Illness: Thresholds Supported Competitive Employment Program

Judith A. Cook, Lisa Razzano

In 1987, Thresholds, a psychosocial rehabilitation agency in Chicago, received a three-year grant from the Robert Wood Johnson Foundation to add supported employment services to its programming for persons with psychiatric disabilities (Cook, 1987). The purpose of this project was to provide community employment and ongoing support to persons with a wide range of psychiatric impairments and diversity of career goals. Thus, we sought to promote permanent or long-term job retention and to

The Thresholds Supported Competitive Employment Program was funded by a grant from the Robert Wood Johnson Foundation, Mental Health Services Development Program, Grant no. 12504. The content of this chapter was developed under a grant from the National Institute on Disability and Rehabilitation Research, Department of Education cooperative agreement no. H133B00011, and the National Institute of Mental Health, Systems Development and Community Support Branch. This chapter does not necessarily reflect the views of the institute and does not imply endorsement by the U.S. government. The authors wish to acknowledge the contributions of Thresholds supervisory staff on the Supported Competitive Employment Program, including Virginia Selleck, associate director, and Jerry Dincin, executive director of Thresholds; the MJSW and Long Term Team staff; Edward Jonas of the Research and Training Center, who prepared portions of the data used in this analysis; Jessica Jonikas of the Research and Training Center, who provided valuable critical assistance; and the members of Thresholds who supported the project and assisted in developing and evaluating the program.

create a model under which clients could receive ongoing vocational support on an as-needed basis. In addition, our solution to this problem addressed clients' requests for quality, community employment that enabled them to interact with nondisabled co-workers in positions that were interesting and esteem-enhancing. In this chapter, we present a description of the program, its implementation, and outcomes of its services. In so doing, we chronicle one agency's attempts to *adapt* supported employment for persons with severe mental illness rather than simply *adopt* a model developed on the basis of experiences with persons who have other types of disabilities.

Background About the Agency

Thresholds is a psychosocial rehabilitation agency located for over thirty years in metropolitan Chicago. Clients, called members, come to the program with an average of six previous psychiatric hospitalizations after many years of illness. In fiscal year 1988 (7/87–6/88), Thresholds provided job support to 410 persons engaged in integrated, community employment, 213 at the agency's north branch and 197 at its south side branch. During any given month of that year, approximately 50 percent of the entire combined membership (including those still in prevocational phases of the program) were employed. Members of the two branches worked at jobs such as factory assembly work, clerical work, janitorial services, food service occupations, housekeeping services, and stock work.

Yet figures from a follow-up of all clients conducted in fiscal year 1988 at six months after they left the program revealed that the percentage employed dropped from 50 percent while in the program to 38 percent after leaving the program. It appeared that clients were unable to maintain the vocational gains they had made, with agency support, after leaving the agency. Moreover, there was evidence that clients benefited from *longer* rather than *shorter* periods of employment support. While 63 percent of those who attended the program for 647 days (the median length of stay in the program) or longer were employed during the follow-up period, only 35 percent of those active in the program for less than 647 days were working. These two findings—that clients benefited from longer periods of vocational support and that their vocational performance worsened once they no longer were receiving services— became important foundations of the supported competitive employment (SCE) model as staff and members developed it.

Previous Literature

Previous research on vocational performance among persons with severe mental illness suggested two issues that should be addressed in formulating programs: transfer of training, and employment as normalization experience. Regarding the first, if the goal is community employment and vocational training takes place in a segregated setting, the client may encounter difficulties in adjusting to a competitive work environment and applying learned skills (Whitehead, 1979; Revell, Wehman, and Arnold, 1984). Concerning the second, work is thought to be a complementary therapeutic goal for those with psychiatric disabilities because of needs for integrated, esteem-enhancing experiences (Lamb, 1979; Kemp and Mercer, 1983; Daniels, Zelman, and Campbell, 1967). It is of great importance, then, to retain those features of the workplace that are shared in common with the nonhandicapped labor force (Roussel and Cook, 1987). Once the conditions of work are organized in a manner that *negates* the status-building aspects of employment, work may cease to function as a rewarding activity for persons with long-term mental illness (Estroff, 1981).

After considering this literature, the question facing our staff was how to design service delivery systems that had two key features: flexibility and permeable programmatic boundaries. In our model-building process, we used the philosophy of not simply *adopting* the supported employment model developed for use with persons who are mentally retarded, but instead *adapting* it for use by our population. There is now an accumulated body of evidence about what vocational principles are effective in transitioning persons with mental illness into paid community employment (Cook, Jonikas, and Solomon, in press), and we felt that we could design a program with these principles in mind. What follows details the central principles we used to create the model, and how these were incorporated in the resulting service delivery system.

Principles of Supported Environment

The first principle was to design a system with maximal flexibility, in order to allow clients the opportunity to help set the pace of their own rehabilitation. This goal called for flexibility in two ways: in an ongoing approach to support that could last as long as the client desired services, and through delivery of services on an as-needed basis so that clients could fade in and out of our program as their needs dictated.

In applying this principle, we were concerned with utilizing supported employment judiciously and economically; by this, we mean we wanted to be able to vary the intensity of services so that we could increase them when needed and decrease them when no longer required. This was done in recognition that, unlike some other handicaps, the course of mental illness is variable and requires vocational services that can be offered on a "prn" or as-needed basis. A corollary to this principle was that the services should be delivered by a group of staff who did not expect a consistent level of client contact but could juggle schedules and coordinate service delivery to meet the waxing and waning needs of their clients for support.

The second principle was to provide the services at the workplace. Primarily, we did this because of the research on transfer of training that indicates the advisability of on-the-job training and support (Bond and Dincin, 1986; Cook, Solomon, and Mock, 1989). Another source of motivation was the knowledge that consumers needed workplace advocacy as well as education of employers, especially to enable natural supports (Cook, Jonikas, and Solomon, forthcoming). Our feeling was that staff who were already on the job site and known to all participants would be in a better position to innovate and intervene in crucial situations. This meant designing staff job objectives so that work-site-based expectations were spelled out clearly, yet allowing staff the freedom to innovate and improvise their own approaches to providing support.

A third principle was to provide services in a nonstigmatizing service delivery context. Several researchers have commented on the preferability of serving clients outside a social service setting, as in university-based transition programs (Unger, Danley, Kohn, and Hutchinson, 1987) and in commercial employment settings (Cook, 1992). Such an approach can help to lessen the stigma attached to this disability, promote normalization, and increase self-esteem. By encouraging clients to meet them for lunch or breakfast near work, or for a "pick-up" game of basketball after work at a nearby gym, staff moved services outside the agency and reinforced regular community socialization. In a similar way, unobtrusive observation of the client at the work site allowed clients to maintain a sense of dignity in front of co-workers, while still affording the MJSW an opportunity to do assessment and intervention.

What was clear to the staff and clients whose feedback was used to develop the model was that program boundaries should be permeable. That is, clients should be able to move from one set of services to another as the needs of their illnesses and career goals dictated. In time, this came to be viewed as an "array of services" model (Cook, Jonikas, and Solomon, in press), in which different types of supports could be accessed by the same individual at different points in his or her lifetime. Rather than trying to develop an approach that was best for everyone, the guiding principle was parsimony, the most efficient utilization of time and material resources by clients on an as-needed basis.

Thresholds Supported Employment Model

Community employment is one of the options Thresholds clients can include in the development of their rehabilitation plans. Although employment is one area in which the agency concentrates its efforts, some clients do not wish to seek employment at the time they enter the program; rather, they turn to Thresholds for social, educational, and residential support. Thus, new clients are placed in programs that fit their needs. For example, at intake clients may report that they do not wish to seek employment but that they would like to meet other clients and engage in leisure and recreational activities. In these cases, clients might consider participating in a nonvocational program. Nonvocational programs place less emphasis on employment issues but will meet the service delivery needs identified by clients. An individual can be a Thresholds client and actively participate in some of the agency rehabilitation services without participation in vocational services.

Although some clients are not interested in vocational services, many others are. At Thresholds, the process by which clients are placed in specific community jobs has several features. After intake, clients interested in vocational services choose to work on one of several crews within the agency (for example, maintenance or kitchen crew). Their participation allows them to gain vocational experience such as working on a team with other clients or practicing different types of job skills. After working on a crew, clients review their vocational goals with their caseworkers. This review includes discussions of the types of vocational placements they would prefer. Once clients and their caseworkers decide that it is time for a vocational placement, this is communicated to the entire treatment team. After team discussion, the clients' cases are presented to the vocational staff, who work with the client to develop an appropriate placement.

Until the advent of the SCE program, Thresholds used a transitional employment (TE) model. TE, the vocational approach used by psychosocial programs starting in 1948 at Fountain House, uses time-limited community job placements at minimum wage or above. The idea is that workers progress through a series of jobs learning new job skills, acquiring a work history, and gaining confidence. A version of this transitional model used at the Thresholds agency involved progressing from a time-limited group placement (where an individual worked with a permanent job coach for minimum wage in a group setting), to a time-limited individual placement (working alone and supervised by the firm's own managers), to a permanent unsupported job found with the help of a job club or job developer through employer-client matching. This TE model was embedded in a program offering an extensive set of services, including social skills, housing and independent living training, leisure and recreation activities, medication management, and education services.

To address needs for ongoing support not met by the TE model, we created a new staff position called the *mobile job support worker* (MJSW) to provide ongoing, mobile support and intervention at the work site or nearby. Delivering services in nonstigmatizing contexts away from the rehabilitation agency, this person was available to assist on an as-needed basis, providing evaluation, training, advocacy with employers and co-workers, and placement.

Another need not met by TE with six-month time limits was for job placements that could be held for longer periods of time. Some clients needed and preferred to remain at the jobs where they were initially placed, or required longer periods before they were ready to move on to more challenging employment. To address this, we removed the time limits for many of our placements so that clients could stay on as full-time employees if they and their employers wished.

The suspension of time limits on job placements, along with MJSW support, became the basis of supported employment services delivered at Thresholds. Through this approach, individuals received ongoing assistance in finding employment and, once on the job, support in maintaining their jobs within integrated work settings.

The overarching goal of Thresholds' Supported Competitive Employment (SCE) Program was to enable persons with severe and persistent mental illness to find and maintain community employment. To that end, eight principal objectives were addressed. The first was delivery of job support services at the workplace or nearby through MJSWs attached to each of the agency's psychosocial teams. The second objective was to design and implement a new long-term program for lower-functioning clients directed at job retention and avoidance of rehospitalization. This involved a third objective of operating a training placement at a neighborhood factory, where long-term clients could gain experience performing paid work similar to tasks they would be doing on their first supported job. Also included was a fourth objective of providing transportation and transportation training to the long-term clients that would enable them to utilize the training placement experience. The fifth objective of our program was to develop a wider range of jobs, particularly individual placements and permanent jobs, which would then be supported by the MJSW working with the psychosocial teams (Cook, 1986).

Along with direct service objectives, an additional objective was to develop an employer marketing module and an employer training manual to be used for job development and employer training. The seventh objective was to disseminate the project through research and training materials and in-person presentations at conferences and training seminars. The eighth and final objective was to create a data set and body of research to address the effectiveness of supported employment services for persons with long-term mental illness (Cook, 1986).

Program Implementation

In the first project year, we hired and trained the project vocational staff, consisting of four MJSWs (one per team for each of the branch's two teams) and six part-time long-term team (LTT) staff (three at each of the two branches). We also reorganized the program at each agency into three components with completely permeable boundaries. One component used a single case manager within a team; the other two components used a "total team" case management approach (Witheridge, Dincin, and Appleby, 1982) with shared case management responsibility.

Vocational Service Components. The first component was the *day program,* composed of interdisciplinary teams of staff assisting members who were working on achieving a series of rehabilitation goals (in addition to employment), which included residential independence, educational attainment, socialization, and avoidance of rehospitalization. These clients attended a five-day-per-week rehabilitation program and received transitional and supported residential services, GED and college preparatory education, individual case management, group counseling, socialization and leisure-time activities, and medication management. To each team, an MJSW was added to provide individual vocational support at or near the workplace or the agency, to develop jobs through client-employer matching, and to run vocational problem-solving groups.

The second component, called *placement only,* was for clients who had achieved desired objectives in the foregoing areas and needed ongoing vocational support to retain the jobs they already had obtained. Services in this component were provided by MJSW staff. Clients came to the agency once a week for an evening program including individual casework, vocational problem-solving groups, and a socialization activity. Clients in this component received additional services at the work site, in the community, or over the telephone as the need arose on a "prn" basis.

The third component, called the *long-term team,* was composed of clients who were already participating in one of the agency's nonvocational programs. This component combined vocational achievement, independent living, and socialization goals. Vocational issues were explored with lower intensity, and clients were welcomed into this program regardless of their stated vocational goals. This program met three times per week at a local church, with a schedule of individual counseling, group problem solving, leisure activities, and career development groups. As a result of participating in the long-term team, many clients made the decision to try working in a community job setting. This component was run by the LTT staff with additional support through MJSWs.

Delivery of mobile job support to clients began in September 1987, and the two long-term teams were formed and operating by November 1987. The training placement at a local factory was started in December of the same year. Implementing this placement included setting up a system for transporting clients to and from the workplace along with conducting travel training for use of public transportation.

Types of Vocational Support Delivered by the Program

Employed clients receiving MJSW support held jobs found on their own as well as placements developed through the agency. Vocational services included job development, job finding assistance, workplace orientation, on-the-job training, job coaching, ongoing support, co-worker and employer involvement, and workplace advocacy. Also offered by the MJSWs was assistance with work-related case management issues such as benefits, medications, or problems with social relationships. For some clients, MJSWs provided services most intensively during the first few weeks on the job and only weekly at the agency thereafter. Other clients needed MJSW involvement throughout their tenure at a position in order to help with difficulties that emerged after a successful vocational adjustment. Still other clients required MJSW services when they lost their jobs through resignations, layoffs, and firings.

The emphasis was on services delivered at the work site itself, but often MJSWs meet with clients outside of their job location. For example, the first few days of a job placement might require some basic skills. If a client had difficulties getting up early on his or her own, a MJSW might arrange a wake-up call and meet the client for breakfast in the community for the first week of a new job. Other clients might have difficulties learning new routes on public transportation or need help completing insurance forms, federal tax forms, or I-9 forms. Finally, job-site orientation often was needed. Depending on previous work history, clients required assistance learning the layout of the building, use of a time clock, break schedules, or the roles of different supervisors or co-workers.

Mobile job support also was beneficial to clients who encountered difficulties at their jobs over the long haul. For example, some supervisors felt that members were performing adequately but could show some improvement. MJSWs worked together with employers and clients to help members understand and meet new job demands and to assist supervisors in communicating expectations to employees.

The mobile nature of intervention was especially important for clients who wanted to keep their disability confidential in order to avoid stigmatization or "special treatment." In these cases, the MJSW met with the client outside of the workplace, at a restaurant or coffee shop or at the agency. Furthermore, MJSWs could visit the job site (if it was a public place such as a supermarket or department store) to make confidential observations of the client's performance.

Finally, MJSWs served as liaisons to employers in order to educate them about some of the needs of their new employees. For example, if a client needed a brief hospitalization yet wanted to return to his or her job, the MJSW could convey these concerns to the employer. Many employers were quite willing to work with an MJSW and were able to accommodate his or her client's needs. Often, educating the employer about mental illness was as essential as direct support to the client to help maintain the job placement.

Two Case Examples. The following examples describe two clients at Thresholds and the types of mobile job support services they received. These examples reveal that the role of the MJSW often includes providing social and relationship support in addition to vocational support services.

Frank was a member of the placement-only component who started a new placement at a local motel as a desk clerk. Over the next few weeks, he contacted his MJSW about several issues. When he started his placement, Frank was anxious about being able to balance the cash register at the end of his shift. He was able to complete this task, but on one occasion made a $40 error. He sought assistance from his MJSW about how to deal with this issue, including whether or not he should simply solve the problem by making up the balance himself and how he should inform his employer about this mistake. A few weeks later, Frank was fired from this position because he disbursed petty cash to a co-worker who did not repay the voucher. He was, however, reinstated because the money was returned. Although Frank was relieved to have his job back, he decided, with the help of his MJSW, that he would not sign out petty cash without approval from his supervisor. In addition to assistance with issues on the job, Frank sought support for other problems. Frank received a letter from an attorney about a student loan on which it was presumed that he had defaulted. The MJSW worked with Frank, Frank's father, and several state and government agencies to help Frank get this loan deferred. Frank's MJSW also helped him file the special paperwork needed to collect SSDI, negotiate a raise with his supervisor, obtain a special users' pass for the public transportation system, and deal with a robbery in one of the rooms at the motel. Frank needed assistance from an MJSW for many social as well as vocational issues. Frank's MJSW spoke with his sister several times and was able to help Frank resolve some conflicts with members of his church, in which Frank was a very active member.

Susan was a member of the placement-only component, enrolled in a secretarial training program from which she was about to graduate. She began to feel pressure about what she would do after graduation: look for a job or attend fashion design school. Susan wanted to go back to school, but she was under considerable pressure from her mother to take a job in order to help pay their monthly expenses. Susan's MJSW helped her with her decision to attend school and work part time. The MJSW also helped her fill out school admissions and financial aid applications and talked to her mother about what types of options Susan had available. Susan decided to take a job as a secretary, but soon quit because she feared learning how to use a computer. She looked for several new jobs but finally returned to her position after she and her MJSW were able to negotiate with her supervisor less use of a computer in her position. She felt much less stress and was more comfortable at her job. Susan also relied on her MJSW for assistance in social matters. She experienced some conflict with a person with whom she was in a relationship and it was affecting her schoolwork. In fact, after she failed a history course, she decided not to continue with this relationship. Once she started her new job, Susan began a new relationship with one of her co-workers. Her MJSW was able to help her to manage this relationship at her workplace as well as set limits.

The logs written by Susan's MJSW reflected issues central to her employment, but they also noted that these new, positive social events had significantly affected Susan's mental health, physical health, and self-esteem. As she became more successful, she encountered more and more challenging life decisions in addition to vocational demands.

Long-Term Services

Unlike those in the day and placement-only components, members in the long-term component often had been unsuccessful in finding and maintaining employment. Yet these clients desired some sort of structured programming. The lower intensity of this component enabled many clients to participate who would not or could not meet the more stringent attendance demands of the day program. The focus in this component was on encouraging vocational achievement by enhancing social and independent living skills and promoting career awareness. Prior to the SCE project, members in these types of programs were assumed to be unable to work. Yet, on opening up vocational opportunities to this group of members, staff discovered that many were interested in and capable of community employment.

One of the biggest challenges in this component was job development; members wanted low-stress positions that were interesting and esteem-enhancing. Several individual and group placements were developed to meet this need but fell short of the mark. Finally, with funding from the Rehabilitative Services Administration of the U.S. Department of Education, the Theater Arts Program evolved (Cook, 1988). This program provided jobs in theaters, theater arts apprenticeships, and acting class scholarships to members with a limited range of vocational abilities.

Jobs held through the Theater Arts Program addressed the need for high-status, high-interest positions for individuals with few trade skills but high levels of artistic creativity. The connection with theater companies and chances to work with professional actors, producers, and directors made these jobs particularly attractive to members. Members also encountered higher-than-average acceptance from their nonhandicapped co-workers, since theater artists seemed to be less fearful of persons with symptoms and impairments related to mental illness. In fact, the actors' ability to see the strengths and artistic abilities of members enabled clients to integrate more fully than in other job settings. By the end of our project, twenty-nine individuals had participated in the Theater Arts Program: fifteen through individual placements and eighteen on crews (with some overlap). Persons on individual placements worked in the box office and concession areas, performed set construction (carpentry and painting), and worked on the companies' running crews (as stagehands, moving and flying sets). Other positions included house manager, assistant director at a theater festival, and dishwasher. Members on crews prepared subscription or advertising mailings and performed maintenance tasks at a number of theaters. Positions ranged from one day in duration (for mailings) to permanent jobs, and work hours were variable, depending on the position, generally ranging from five to twenty hours per week, with some full-time work.

Two Case Examples. The emphasis in the long-term team component was on relating real-world phenomena to employment and on teaching independence through problem solving and skill development. As the following examples illustrate, clients in the long-term program often reached rehabilitation goals in their own unique manner.

> The long-term team staff had been driving members to the training placement at a local factory and then providing vocational support on the job. The members were told by the staff that the following week they would be expected to use public transportation to travel to work, and that they would need to be on time, even when they were responsible for getting to work on their own. The next day, staff noticed that some of the members they usually drove to work were not at the agreed-on pickup site. When the group arrived at the work site, they found that these members were already on the job, working at their stations. They had decided to surprise the staff by trying public transportation on their own.

> Bernard was a member who worked at a factory enclave at a light manufacturing plant in Chicago. An outgoing and personable individual, Bernard had difficulty limiting the amount of socializing he did on the job. Despite repeated warnings from MJSWs to do less talking to his co-workers and more work, Bernard's speed and work quality were

still far below industrial rate. At the same time, Bernard was attending a vocational problem-solving skills group offered by the long-term team component. Here, the focus was on helping members learn to think about their problems and construct their own solutions. All this seemed to have little impact on Bernard until he came to group one day and proudly related that he had solved his "talking problem." By requesting a seat change on the production line, Bernard was now sitting between two hearing impaired co-workers. "I couldn't talk to them even if I wanted to," he exclaimed. One potential problem was Bernard's stated desire to learn sign language.

Empirical Findings

In this section, we summarize our empirical findings.

Service Utilization. Over the three years of the project, a total of 1,170 clients received services through the SCE program. In all, 807 clients received services while members of the day program, 233 clients received services on long-term teams, and 130 clients were served while members of the placement-only program. Many clients received more than one type of SCE service. A total of 561 clients received one or more instances of support from the project MJSWs. A total of 1,017 clients attended vocational problem-solving and training groups run by RWJF-funded staff. Of those served in the program, the proportion employed averaged 81.9 percent over the thirty-six months of the project period. Two projectwide client satisfaction surveys (Brown, 1989; Jonas, 1990) indicated a high level of satisfaction among project clients with the type and effectiveness of services they were receiving.

Characteristics of Members in SCE Components. The demographic characteristics of members in the three SCE program components were highly similar. Day program members were slightly younger (average age = thirty-three years) than placement-only and long-term team members (average age = thirty-five years). Day program and placement-only members averaged thirteen years of education, while the long-term team members averaged twelve years. The gender distribution of the three components also was similar, with 68 percent male/32 percent female in the day program, 60 percent male/40 percent female in placement-only, and 66 percent male/34 percent female in the long-term teams. Fifty-eight percent of members in day and placement-only components were members of minority groups, while the proportion of minorities in long-term teams was lower, at 40 percent.

Regarding illness histories, more differences were apparent. While day and placement-only members had been hospitalized for psychiatric reasons an average of four times, long-term team members had been hospitalized an average of six times. When comparing the total number of months members had been hospitalized for psychiatric reasons, members in the long-term teams averaged the highest number (25 months), followed by placement-only (19 months), and day program members (11.6 months). Similarly, members of long-term teams had been ill for an average of 6.3 years, while members in the day program had been ill an average of 4.7 years. Interestingly, members in placement-only had been ill the longest, an average of 11.2 years, despite having fewer hospitalizations and fewer months hospitalized in their lifetimes. Finally, members were first hospitalized, on average, at age twenty-eight in the day and long-term components, and at age 24 among placement-only members.

Regarding work history, members of placement-only and the long-term teams had the highest numbers of days worked at longest job ever held (an average of thirty-seven months), while day program members had the lowest (an average of twenty-eight months). This was unexpected for long-term team members, who were lower functioning and who sought out programming of lower intensity. Once we examined the Hollingshead occupational prestige scores of members in the three components, however, the reason became apparent. While they may have had longer job histories, long-term team members had longest jobs of lower prestige, averaging a score of 66 on the Hollingshead (in the range of semiskilled and unskilled employees) as compared to averages of 58 for day program and 52 for placement-only (in the range of skilled manual employees). Thus, while long-term team members had longer jobs, they held positions of lower prestige and corresponding income and education levels.

Nature of Vocational Supports. All project staff documented the vocational support they provided using a logging system developed for this purpose (Cook, 1987). This method involved recording the type of support, where it occurred, who it involved, the type of work setting and employer, the amount of travel time and length of the support event, and a narrative description of the nature of the intervention. Each support event was coded separately if the type of contact changed (such as from an in-person meeting to a phone call) and if the type of person changed (for example, an MJSW working alongside a member and then meeting separately with the member's supervisor).

Altogether, 6,664 logged instances of support were recorded during the three-year project period. The largest number of supports were delivered to clients in the day program (2,585 supports), followed in frequency by supports to members in the long-term team (N = 2,174) and the fewest number of supports to members in placement-only (N = 1,633). The large majority (77 percent or 5,164 supports) were in-person meetings, while a fifth of all supports (21 percent) involved phone calls made or received by the MJSW. Only 1 percent of all supports involved nonroutine paperwork.

Regarding employment status at the time support was delivered, 43 percent (N = 2,857) of all supports went to members on group placements, 36 percent (N = 2,398) was received by members in competitive jobs, 12 percent (N = 802) of all supports went to unemployed members, 7 percent (N = 472) of supports went to members on individual placements, and 1 percent (N = 48) went to those working in the training enclave. The mean length of supports was 26.6 minutes, and the average travel time involved in supports was 55 minutes (for those supports requiring travel). Travel occurred in 33 percent of *all* supports and 55 percent of all *first* supports. The number of supports received by an individual ranged from 1 to 124, with an average of 12 supports per member. Interestingly, while the MJSW was originally developed to handle emergencies, only 2 percent of all supports (N = 126) were judged to involve emergencies, defined as any situation that was life threatening (to a member or those around the member), job threatening, or likely to result in rehospitalization.

Length of Support by Work Status and Intervention Type. Table 2.1 presents the average length of vocational supports (in minutes) by type of employment status. The average length of support events ranged from a low of fifteen minutes (for unemployed long-term team members) to a high of forty-four minutes (among day program members on individual placements). In all three program components, the average support event was longer for members on individual placements than on any other type of employment. This is not surprising, given that this step involves working without the presence of other members and without a job coach for support. Interestingly, the average length of support events for independent jobs did not vary widely by program, averaging twenty-five minutes for members in the day program and twenty-two minutes for those in placement-only and the long-term teams. These averages indicate that support does not fade as members' jobs increase in complexity and independence, but that members require longer periods of support as they make the step from a group to an individual job setting.

Table 2.1. Clients' Average Support in
Minutes Per Contact by Job Status and Program

Job Status	Program		
	Day program	Placement only	Long-term team
Unemployed	33.8	20.3	15.3
Group placement	34.0	21.9	17.8
Individual placement	44.6	40.0	24.7
Independent job	25.7	22.7	22.2
Training enclave		18.8	13.6

Table 2.2 presents the average support time by the nature of the intervention. Here, the lengthiest supports for members in the day and placement-only components involved an *active intervention* to address a member's job problem (for example, working alongside the member, meeting with the member's supervisor). This was not the case for members in the long-term team, for whom *job finding* and *verbal reassurance about vocational issues* involved the longest average support times.

Amount of Support Needed by Member Characteristics. Another question was whether or not members with different types of demographic, work history, and illness features received different total amounts of support time. Total support time was calculated by summing the amount of time for each support event received by a member. The average total amount of time received was highest among members in placement-only (614 minutes or 10.2 hours), followed by day program (318 minutes or 5.3 hours) and long-term team members (245 minutes or 4.1 hours).

No relationships were found between members' characteristics and total support time for day program members. Among placement-only members, those with longer illnesses received more total support time ($r = .56$, $p < .01$), as did those who were older ($r = .64$, $p < .01$), and white members received more support than minority members ($r = .43$, $p < .05$). This pattern was reversed among members of long-term teams, where members who were older at their first psychiatric hospitalization and those with shorter rather than longer illnesses received significantly more total support time ($r = .33$ and $4 = -.28$ respectively, $p < .05$).

Summary and Conclusions

Our experiences in designing and implementing the SCE program have taught us many valuable lessons about the nature of vocational support needed by persons with long-term mental illness. Some of these lessons are documented with empirical data, but we need much more research

Table 2.2. Clients' Average Support in
Minutes Per Contact by Support Type and Program

Support Type	Program		
	Day program	*Placement only*	*Long-term team*
Casework problem	24.1	22.1	15.6
Verbal job support	25.9	26.2	21.0
Job problem	42.0	36.9	18.6
Job finding problem	33.2	30.2	21.1
Other type of support	33.7	22.4	18.0

before we can affirm them as generalizable principles. First, different types of populations with mental illness appear to require different types and amounts of employment support. This was evident in the case of long-term team clients, who had been viewed as incapable of community employment before the project began. These members were able to work but needed to get ready at their own pace and needed jobs of fewer hours per week, requiring development of low stress, lower-skilled positions. Yet long-term team members also needed interesting, esteem-enhancing work as well as co-workers who were accepting and open to integration at the work site.

Another valuable lesson concerned the nature of supports needed by members. While the vast majority of interventions were face to face, a considerable amount of phone calling (a fifth of all supports) occurred in the project. The telephone was an effective instrument for handling interactions with employers who were too busy to meet in person with MJSWs. It also provided a convenient "check-in" format for members who did not wish to travel to the agency but needed ongoing reassurance after work or on weekends. This is an example of adapting the supported employment model to meet the needs of persons with mental illness for support on an as-needed basis in a nonstigmatizing context.

Travel time was revealed to be a major expenditure of staff effort on this project. This came as no surprise, given the emphasis on *mobile* support delivered at the *workplace* or elsewhere in the *community*. It is interesting to note that the average length of travel time (fifty-five minutes) was *longer* than support time (twenty-six minutes). Also, travel occurred in one-third of all support instances and over half (55 percent) of all *first* supports to members (for example, in going to see the member's work site, meeting the member's supervisor). As a frequently occurring type of support, travel may be a "hidden" expense in many programs that are unaware of the demands it will make on staff time and program costs.

Regarding the *length* of vocational supports, the longest average support times were for members working on individual placements, regardless of the program component in which they participated. With the absence of an agency job coach and other member co-workers for support, individual placements are the step most closely approximating competitive employment. Since average support time on individual placements was longer than for group placements or independent jobs for all three components, this suggests that the need for support does not fade as members assume jobs with increasing autonomy and complexity.

Moreover, for day program and placement-only members, the longest average support times occurred when the MJSW was *actively intervening* in a job problem. This often involved extensive travel to the job site, including observation, identification of the problem, and then retraining. On the other hand, long-term members' longest average supports were for verbal *reassurance* and *job finding*. The high amount of reassurance documented in the logs may be related to the finding that long-term team clients with shorter illnesses of more recent onset required more help adjusting to their newly acquired disability as they entered community employment. Similarly, the large number of job finding activities for long-term members may be related to the needs of this population for continual job development through employer-client matching, with an eye to the needs for low-stress yet interesting work situations. The less challenging nature of these positions may mean that more ambitious job development and less workplace-based intervention is needed. Awareness of this finding may help administrators better plan the staffing needs of programs seeking to serve lower-functioning mental health clients.

Shifting our emphasis away from average length to total amount of support received by members, clients in the placement-only component averaged the highest total number of hours of support. Day and long-term team members received less than half this average. The support needs of placement-only members are especially important, given that they were vocationally successful by definition (that is, those clients with long job tenure yet with needs for ongoing support) and had the least programmatic structure of any of the components. Older members of the placement-only program who had longer illnesses required significantly more support than younger members with illnesses of shorter duration. Among the competitively successful employees, those with more severe illness histories seem to require the most support. Thus, even as members succeed vocationally, success may bring its own set of social and interpersonal demands that require case management–type support. Such needs could be beyond the case management capacity of vocational staff, suggesting the importance of clinical training for MJSWs.

These findings point to the conclusion that vocational support for persons with long-term mental illness is more than skills training and workplace support. The need to attend to developmental issues (Selleck, 1987; Simmons, Selleck, Sepetauc, and Steele, in press) accompanying vocational *success* means that clients' social and interpersonal support needs may grow as they experience vocational achievement. This notion is tied to the nature of rehabilitation as a multidimensional process, in which positive changes in one area may be accompanied by negative changes in another or no change at all. The need for multidimensional outcome models (Anthony and Farkas, 1982) to capture these changes is clear if we hope to understand that rehabilitation outcomes do not all change in the same direction in "successful" situations.

To some extent, this was not "news" to the supervisors and staff of this agency. Their preexisting psychosocial service delivery model makes a theoretical assumption that persons with this disability need lifelong supports, exemplified by the holistic conception of service recipients as "members" rather than solely as clients. Yet it may be a new insight to public funding agencies, especially those with a funding structure that assumes a time-limited need for support delivered through a process of continual "fading." In light of these observations, we may need to re-think at least two fairly standard assumptions of vocational rehabilita-tion: first, that clients need support for a time-limited period, after which they should be "closed"; and second, that support needs "fade" in a simple linear fashion over time on the job. We already have begun to question the first assumption in the debate over who is responsible for long-term support in supported employment. Perhaps a lifelong succes-sion of "fadings" is a better way to conceptualize the needs of persons with psychiatric disability throughout their employment careers.

Finally, the finding that support needs are different for different groups of people suggests that we need vocational programming capable of providing an array of services for persons with psychiatric disability. Just how to do this in today's economy and funding climate is a major question now facing the field. The agency in question has been able to continue many SCE positions beyond the period of Robert Wood John-son funding. This has involved reallocation of existing funds for voca-tional staff in light of the benefits perceived in the outcomes resulting from these new services and staff functions. In an era of "downsizing," however, these positions run the risk of elimination, and this points to the need for rigorous research to test their effectiveness.

By embarking on a new wave of program development, one psychosocial rehabilitation agency in Chicago altered its TE program-ming to meet the needs of a wider range of clients. In doing so, an array of supports became available, incorporating several principles that bear further scrutiny. As others investigate these principles, the increased knowledge that results can be used to refine and better utilize these ideas in new programming for persons with mental illness.

References

Anthony, W. A., and Farkas, M. "A Client Outcome Planning Model for Assessing Psychi-atric Rehabilitation Interventions." *Schizophrenia Bulletin*, 1982, 8, 13–38.

Bond, G. R., and Dincin, J. "Accelerating Entry into Transitional Employment in a Psychosocial Rehabilitation Agency." *Rehabilitation Psychology*, 1986, 31, 143–155.

Brown, R. *Report to Members and Staff Regarding Client Satisfaction Survey for the First Year of the Supported Competitive Employment Program.* Chicago: Thresholds Research Insti-tute, 1989.

Cook, J. A. *Thresholds Supported Competitive Employment Program for Persons with Severe and Persistent Mental Illness.* Grant no. 12504. Proposal to the Robert Wood Johnson Foundation, Princeton, N.J., 1986.

Cook, J. A. *Instructions for Completing the Supported Competitive Employment Log.* Chicago: Thresholds Research Institute, 1987.

Cook, J. A. *Vocational Opportunities in the Theater Arts for Persons with Severe and Persistent Mental Illness.* Grant no. H128A91014. Proposal to the U.S. Department of Education, Washington, D.C., 1988.

Cook, J. A. "Job Ending Among Youth and Adults with Severe Mental Illness." *Journal of Mental Health Administration,* 1992, *19* (2), 158–169.

Cook, J. A., Jonikas, J., and Solomon, M. "Models of Vocational Rehabilitation for Youth and Adults with Severe Mental Illness: Research and Service Delivery." *American Rehabilitation,* in press.

Cook, J. A., Solomon, M., and Mock, L. "What Happens After the First Job Placement: Vocational Transitioning Among Severely Emotionally Disturbed and Behavior Disordered Adolescents." *Programming for Adolescents with Behavioral Disorders,* 1989, *4,* 71–93.

Daniels, D. N., Zelman, A. B., and Campbell, J. H. "Community-Based Task Groups in Recovery of Mental Patients." *Archives of General Psychiatry,* 1967, *16,* 215–228.

Estroff, S. E. *Making It Crazy.* Berkeley: University of California Press, 1981.

Jonas, E. *Report to Members and Staff Regarding Client Satisfaction Survey for the Second Year of the Supported Competitive Employment Program.* Chicago: Thresholds Research Institute, 1990.

Kemp, H. J., and Mercer, A. "Unemployment, Disability, and Rehabilitation Centers and Their Effects on Mental Health." *Journal of Occupational Therapy,* 1983, *56,* 37–48.

Lamb, H. R. "Roots of Neglect of the Long-Term Mentally Ill." *Psychiatry,* 1979, *42,* 452–468.

Revell, G., Wehman, P., and Arnold, S. "Supported Work Model of Competitive Employment for Persons with Mental Retardation: Implications of Rehabilitative Services." *Journal of Rehabilitation,* 1984, *50,* 33–38.

Roussel, A., and Cook, J. A. "The Role of Work in Psychiatric Rehabilitation: The Visiting Chefs Program as an Alternative to Competitive Employment." *Sociological Practice,* 1987, *6,* 149–168.

Selleck, V. "Social Networks and Dropping Out of Psychiatric Rehabilitation: Exploring the Relationship." Unpublished doctoral dissertation, Department of Counseling Psychology, School of Education and Social Policy, Northwestern University, 1987.

Simmons, T., Selleck, V., Sepetauc, F., and Steele, R. "Psychiatric Vocational Rehabilitation: A Puzzle with Several Pieces." In R. W. Flexer and P. Solomon (eds.), *Community and Social Support for People with Severe Mental Disabilities: Service Integration in Rehabilitation and Mental Health.* San Francisco: Jossey-Bass, in press.

Unger, K., Danley, K., Kohn, L., and Hutchinson, D. "Rehabilitation Through Education: Program for Young Adults with Psychiatric Disabilities on a University Campus." *Psychosocial Rehabilitation Journal,* 1987, *10,* 35–49.

Whitehead, C. "Sheltered Workshops in the Decade Ahead: Work and Wages or Welfare?" In G. T. Bellamy, G. O'Connor, and O. C. Karen (eds.), *Vocational Rehabilitation of Severely Handicapped Individuals.* Baltimore: University Park Press, 1979.

Witheridge, T. F., Dincin, J., and Appleby, L. "Working with the Most Frequent Recidivists: A Total Team Approach to Assertive Resource Management." *Psychosocial Rehabilitation Journal,* 1982, *5,* 9–11.

JUDITH A. COOK is director of the Thresholds National Research and Training Center on Rehabilitation and Mental Illnesses in Chicago.

LISA RAZZANO is principal investigator for the Thresholds National Research and Training Center on Rehabilitation and Mental Illnesses in Chicago.

The development of a community program as a component of a state hospital has succeeded in providing community mental health services in a previously underserved area and has had beneficial effects within the hospital itself.

State Hospital Operation of a Community Program

Carl A. Cappello, Howard D. Reid, John H. Simsarian

Connecticut Valley Hospital (CVH), located in Middletown, Connecticut, was founded through the influence of Dorothea Dix in 1867. Since its establishment, the hospital has gone through many phases, with its patient population peaking at approximately 3,350 in 1940. The 1991 census of 385 patients with inpatient status is the lowest since 1874. With the development of community-based comprehensive mental health service systems, the hospital admission rate has dropped to approximately one-third of its 1986 level of 1,000 a year, and the hospital census has declined by 165 patients during the same period.

CVH has played a significant role in decreasing the inpatient census by reorganizing to facilitate patient movement to less restrictive settings. The hospital has also been a direct force in the development of alternatives to inpatient care by creating an innovative comprehensive community mental health center, River Valley Services, serving the immediate area in which the hospital is located.

As the primary locus of public mental health care has shifted from the state hospital to community programs, the role and future of state hospitals have been brought into question. The development of River Valley Services by CVH represents one innovative approach to the evolving role of the state hospital and the integration of hospital resources into the broader service system.

This chapter describes the development of River Valley Services and the implications of the program for a state psychiatric hospital operating a comprehensive community mental health center. It sketches the systemic and administrative context for the development of the center and describes the development process itself. Finally, the chapter reviews the implications of the program for the larger hospital organization of which it is a component.

Context for Program Development

In 1983, the Connecticut Department of Mental Health issued a comprehensive plan that defined the department's "target population" as people with severe mental illness and provided a blueprint for the development of comprehensive community-based services. Albeit belatedly, Connecticut began an expansion of community-based services. This service expansion took place in the organizational context of five geographical regions and twenty-three service catchment areas. The South Central Connecticut Region, with a population of approximately 790,000, is composed of six catchment areas and is the primary source of Connecticut Valley Hospital admissions.

The development of "managed service systems" at a regional and area level began to take shape in 1987 with the development of "lead agencies" in each catchment area in the South Central Region. These area service systems are organized within a broader regional system that includes CVH. The service area in which CVH is located (Catchment Area 10) is comprised of Middletown, with a population of approximately 44,000, and surrounding Middlesex County, with a total population of approximately 140,000. The services within Catchment Area 10 were fragmented and had limited coordination and continuity of care among community service providers and between community programs and the state hospitals. At times, patients left the hospital without adequate community discharge plans, and the residential program serving the area had a reputation of accepting patients who were "easy to handle," regardless of their community of origin. The fragmented nature of these services was frustrating to patients, family members, service providers, and the community at large. Middletown residents were concerned that patients were being admitted to Connecticut Valley Hospital from across the state and then discharged into the Middletown area without adequate supports.

Thus, the Middletown area was a classic "nonsystem" of mental health care, as Stein (1989, p. 29) notes, "where a few patients got more than they needed, many patients got less than they needed, and some got nothing at all. Patients commonly got lost in this nonsystem, with no one feeling obligated to seek them out."

The regional administration of the Department of Mental Health, with support of the regional citizen advisory structure, targeted the Middlesex County area for new case management and crisis intervention funding contingent on services being delivered according to the principles of a managed service system. These principles—which are based on the work of Stein and others—include the following:

Individual client assessments and service plans must be developed that address human needs such as shelter, food, money, social relations, vocation/avocation status, and medical and mental status.

Client needs must be supported over the long term with flexibility.

The client should be supported within a community context recognizing the importance of natural support systems.

The service system must ensure that the services provided are coordinated and integrated.

Services must be responsive, relevant, and accessible. This necessitates the provision of active outreach.

There must be a clearly defined point of accountability for service delivery to ensure that the service system principles are addressed for each client. There must also be the administrative authority to ensure coordination and cooperation between systems components.

Program Development

In 1986, Middlesex County, with its insufficient and fragmented services, had an admission rate and an average daily census at state psychiatric hospitals that were among the highest in the state. Through the actions of a local legislator who recognized the absence of adequate services, the 1986–87 Connecticut budget appropriated new funding for a crisis intervention center for the county as well as for a pilot case management program that would place case managers in each of the South Central Region's catchment areas. While these funds for the county promised to form the core of an adequate service system, there was no local mental health provider strongly interested in developing these programs under the principles of a managed system of care.

Taube and Goldman (1989) have noted that in the early twentieth century, state hospitals took the lead in the mental hygiene movement by developing aftercare clinics in their communities. Connecticut Valley Hospital had for many years provided the largest outpatient clinic for individuals with long-term mental illness in Middlesex County. In the absence of a logical alternate community provider, Connecticut Valley Hospital responded to the call by the Connecticut Department of Mental Health to establish a comprehensive community component to serve only Middlesex County. With consultation from an experienced community program director, the directors of the hospital's clinical departments designed the new entity, River Valley Services, to receive the new funding, in combination with the existing outpatient clinic and projected reallocation of existing hospital resources. The proposal won the support of the Department of Mental Health, and early in 1988 the first new staff members were hired.

The original program configuration for River Valley Services consisted of the outpatient clinic, a case management program (opened in the fall of 1988), and a Mobile Crisis Team (opened in January 1989), which included both a four-bed crisis unit and an outreach-oriented emergency services team. Evening and night shift staffing of the crisis unit would be provided by closing an inpatient ward of Connecticut Valley Hospital and transferring staff on those shifts to River Valley Services.

Recognizing that the original service configuration was inadequate without an intensive community treatment team based on the principles of the Training in Community Living Model (TCL) of Stein and Test (1980), River Valley Services successfully sought funding through the Mental Health Services Development Program of the Robert Wood Johnson Foundation to support the opening of Middlesex Program for Assertive Community Treatment (M-PACT) in August 1989. In addition to establishing these new programs, River Valley Services was designated the "Lead Agency" for the catchment area by the regional director of the Department of Mental Health in January 1990. This gave River Valley Services the responsibility for coordinating and overseeing all Department of Mental Health–funded services in the area (there being no county governance in Connecticut).

By the beginning of 1990, Connecticut Valley Hospital had thus been able to put in place most of the elements considered critical to a comprehensive community support system for the catchment area in which it was located: outreach-oriented clinical and case management services, a TCL-type program to treat individuals needing the most support, a twenty-four-hour, seven-day-per-week comprehensive emergency services program, and a local mental health authority charged with the responsibility of making the system work on behalf of its clients. The new state-operated mental health center was integrated with both the inpatient programs and existing community grant-funded programs. New services developed by these agencies included a social club and rehabilitation programs, new community residences and supervised apartment services, additional outreach-oriented case management services, and supported employment services.

Implementation Issues and Strategies. A number of unique implementation issues were presented in this development. It was imperative that a well-trained, enthusiastic, and committed staff be recruited, and all staff recruitment had to be consistent with civil service regulations and state hospital personnel procedures. Additionally, one of the goals of the development was to retrain existing state hospital staff for employment in community settings. State hospital staff knew the client population well but were inexperienced in community treatment. Although the River Valley Services leadership staff was selected from outside the hospital, encouragement was given to hire a mixture of state hospital employees seeking transfer to the new program and individuals experienced in community settings. In recruiting program staff, the emphasis was placed on selecting individuals who possessed the skills and positive personal values important to the work. These selection criteria are not completely reflected in civil service examinations and collective bargaining agreements. Therefore, the support of personnel officers and careful attention to the interviewing and credential review processes were essential to successful recruitment. The outcome was a direct program staff composed almost equally of former state hospital and nonhospital staff.

Currently, a third of the River Valley Services staff members came to the program from the hospital. River Valley Services has benefited greatly from their knowledge of the client population. Also, their history with "team" models of staffing in the inpatient service has in many cases made it easier for them to acclimate to team models of service delivery in the outpatient setting than it would have been for employees accustomed to an individual clinician model.

Staff reporting and authority relationships had to be examined as well. The hospital is organized by clinical departments, and all supervisory authority falls within these departments. This structure was deemed unworkable for the community program setting in which staff members from various disciplines need to be supervised within their new program. Protracted negotiations occurred concerning the respective roles of the hospital clinical department heads and the River Valley Services community program directors. An accord was finally reached that gave program directors direct supervision of their staff and gave to clinical department heads the authority to determine credentialing standards and to monitor professional practices.

In a similar way, a number of other organizational structures within the hospital had to be modified to support the community program development, often causing significant discussion and negotiation. The budget and accounting system of the hospital was not designed to facilitate program-specific budgeting and expense accounting. As a result, the original estimates of the cost of River Valley Services were significantly underprojected, and it has continued to be difficult to develop accounting systems that accurately monitor costs. Similarly, the majority of hospital policies and procedures were inapplicable to the community program setting, and many policies and procedures necessary in the community did not exist in the hospital manual and had to be developed. Clinical governance remains an unresolved issue, since the hospital structures do not allow for substantial involvement in policy-making by community program staff who have the most expertise in outpatient community mental health services.

There were also a number of unique implementation issues relating to the interface between the hospital and the community. Relationships between the professional mental health and health care agencies within Middlesex County and the hospital had been strained in the several years preceding the development of River Valley Services. Concern was particularly focused around access to the hospital and the perceived "dumping" of patients into the community. There was substantial skepticism among community agencies as to the hospital's ability to adequately administer an important community program. Even among independent mental health advocates, there was considerable concern that the hospital could not truly represent community interests. Thus, much attention during the development phase had to be paid to developing collaborative relationships with community agencies and advocates and to establishing mutual agendas and means of communication. River Valley Services also made it a priority to ensure immediate access to inpatient care when needed, a critical step that supported the program's commitment to respond to community needs. Establishing a community advisory board and maintaining consistent contacts with existing mental health advocacy groups also worked to bridge this gap.

Initial Results. The results of this experiment in evolving state hospital programming have been overwhelmingly positive for Middlesex County Services and for the clients they serve. For the first time, all of the Department of Mental Health–funded programs in the area are working together as part of a system of care, and data reflect these changes. The county's average inpatient census at Connecticut Valley Hospital has been reduced by 40 percent. Admissions have also been reduced by 40 percent. The homeless shelter administration also reports that use of the shelter by individuals with mental illness—once a substantial problem in the county—has been significantly reduced. Access to needed acute care and the working relationship with the general hospital emergency room have both improved substantially. Relationships with the city government, including the police department, are now positive, and even within the downtown business community, there is now greater understanding and less negativism toward mental health clients and programs. The county's residential services (group homes and supported apartments), with the advent of twenty-four hour support from the crisis team, are effectively serving clients with a greater range of treatment needs, and collaboration between the residential provider and the outpatient and inpatient clinical teams has improved markedly. The hospital census decrease that has followed these developments is now making it possible to reallocate funds previously devoted to inpatient care to create new supervised apartment services and to increase staffing for existing residential services. A strong consumer empowerment and support network has formed. Advocacy groups and boards of directors have largely united behind support for a strong community service system, a system in which the hospital is seen as a positive and active player.

Larger Implications

The development of a community mental health program as a component of Connecticut Valley Hospital instead of as a freestanding community mental health provider has implications for both program and hospital, and, in some cases, for the Department of Mental Health as a whole. Most of these implications are positive, but some are negative.

The creation of River Valley Services from a century-old state hospital demonstrated to patients, staff, and the community that the hospital is an active and relevant player in a rapidly changing system of services. There was and continues to be a sense of pride from within the organization that the hospital is vital and moving in new directions while the inpatient service is shrinking. From its inception, River Valley Services has had little difficulty in recruiting staff, many of whom have been long-term employees of the inpatient hospital.

The establishment of a managed system of mental health care in the catchment area immediately surrounding the hospital reinforced for hospital staff and community providers the value of offering treatment in the least restrictive setting and using the community as the primary locus of care.

In addition, this new program was given a mission that was consistent with that of the hospital to provide treatment to persons suffering from severe and prolonged mental illness. It also demonstrated to hospital and community staff throughout the region the interrelatedness of the community program and hospital in a regional mental health system.

The orientation of the hospital staff to serve seriously mentally ill persons was clearly in place and created a common and clear agenda for the new program. The mission and these values are emphasized continually in clinical and administrative settings within the hospital as staff from River Valley Services participate in hospitalwide administrative and clinical structures.

Hospital and Community Relations. As previously mentioned, River Valley Services is committed to responding to the community's needs. Its work demonstrates to the community that patients are not simply being discharged from the hospital and forgotten, but rather that the hospital is actively serving these patients through mobile and assertive community treatment. In 1989, a patient who had escaped from the hospital committed a murder. There was significant expression of community concern over this tragedy. River Valley Services was called on by the mayor to provide crisis counseling to persons in the community who were dealing with the trauma of this event and acted as the hospital's bridge to the community, the police, the business community, and the community general hospital. River Valley Services has continued to receive favorable press coverage in the local newspaper as it has expanded services and implemented assertive community treatment over the past two years, thus significantly contributing to the hospital's community relations.

Budgetary Implications. The years 1983 through 1989 were financially strong years for the state, which allowed for major expansion of community services and the resulting decrease in inpatient services. A major factor in the establishment of River Valley Services was the hospital's ability to redirect resources from its inpatient service in combination with new funding.

In contrast, 1990 and 1991 were years of recession and large budget deficits in Connecticut. Connecticut Valley Hospital has been significantly affected by this deficit. River Valley Services, while previously the recipient of reallocated staff positions, now is subject to these same budget restrictions. The reality of diminished resources within the hospital is greater competition for remaining resources among all components of the hospital, including River Valley Services. River Valley Services is small and vulnerable when compared with the inpatient service, and without continuing support from the larger organization, its ability to perform its role in the community could be seriously threatened.

The Bureaucracy. Operating as a state agency can bring with it the benefits of structure; however, when developing new and creative community services, working with the established state administrative system within the hospital and beyond has been challenging. Developing an innovative program has forced a review of the "this is the way we have always done it" approach, which has been beneficial to the broader system by facilitating a more critical review of existing practices and forcing an element of flexibility. This process has been time consuming and has required creativity on the part of the management of River Valley Services, the hospital, and the state administration. Some specific examples of how the administrative structure impedes program development include the following:

1. The current clinical governance structure of the hospital is limited to physicians and therefore does not formally include multidisciplinary staff at River Valley Services in clinical policy-making.
2. All revenues generated by River Valley Services accrue to the state general fund and cannot be used for providing expanded mental health services.
3. Due to budgetary and administrative constraints, River Valley Services has been unable to lease space in the downtown Middletown

area and has remained on the hospital grounds. The state hospital location has negative implications for many patients and makes access to the site difficult.

State Employee Unions. Connecticut has a long tradition of strong state employee unions. The state engages in collective bargaining, including binding arbitration for settling contract disputes.

In Connecticut, large state agencies such as the Department of Mental Health and the Department of Mental Retardation directly run state hospitals, training schools, and other institutions, utilizing state employees. Community-based services such as outpatient clinics and community residential programs may be either state operated or provided by nonprofit agencies utilizing state grant funds. Many of these nonprofit providers are nonunion, and even those that have become unionized frequently cannot match the salaries and fringe benefits earned by state workers performing similar tasks. Thus, state employee unions view the private nonprofit sector as both a threat to their hard-won benefits and an opportunity for expanding membership to these agencies.

The development of River Valley Services as a component of the state hospital presented an opportunity to the unions to expand their membership into community-based services while simultaneously protecting the jobs of state employees working at a state hospital that was downsizing. The result is a working partnership that has contributed to the success of River Valley Services from its inception to the present. More important, it continues to serve as an example of job creation for the Department of Mental Health as it reduces its inpatient services.

Conclusion

The development of River Valley Services as a component of Connecticut Valley Hospital has been highly successful in providing a comprehensive community mental health center within a previously underserved area. In addition to the actual service delivery, there have been major administrative and fiscal advantages for both the program and the hospital. Often, what would have been considered disadvantageous, such as resistance to administrative change and policy inconsistencies between inpatient and community programs, may be considered in a broader context as beneficial to the vitality of the state hospital. The hospital must be responsive to changes over time in the systems of which it is an integral part.

References

Stein, L. I. "Wisconsin's System of Mental Health Financing." In D. Mechanic and L. H. Aiken (eds.), *Paying for Services: Promises and Pitfalls of Capitation.* New Directions for Mental Health Services, no. 43. San Francisco: Jossey-Bass, 1989.

Stein, L. I., and Test, M. A. "Alternative to Mental Hospital Treatment, I: Conceptual Model, Treatment Program, and Clinical Evaluation." *Archives of General Psychiatry,* 1980, *37,* 392–397.

Taube, C. A., and Goldman, H. H. "State Strategies to Restructure Psychiatric Hospitals: A Selective Review." *Inquiry,* 1989, *26,* 146–156.

CARL A. CAPPELLO *is superintendent of Connecticut Valley Hospital, Middletown, Connecticut.*

HOWARD D. REID *is director of River Valley Services, Connecticut Valley Hospital, Middletown, Connecticut.*

JOHN H. SIMSARIAN *is the Department of Mental Health regional director for South Central Connecticut.*

A supported housing program should meet the needs of its clients for a home in the context of a supportive community.

The Clustered Apartment Project: A Conceptually Coherent Supported Housing Model

Lawrence Telles

A supported housing program for those with a serious psychiatric disability should provide dependable social support and a stable housing situation for its clientele. This combined area is best thought of as the provision of a home in the context of a supportive community. Decisions about program design and client characteristics should reflect that intent.

Home means housing in the context of neighborhood, family, and friends. It implies comfort, safety, stability. "Home is the place where, when you have to go there, they have to take you in." Home is where you do not need to "prepare a face to meet the faces that you meet." Etymologically, *home* (dwelling) means both a place within which one can linger and from which one can wander and return (Cooper, 1989). If the term were not already used to mean the *house*less, it would be clearest to call supported housing programs: programs for the *home*less.

Some of the people who need intensive psychosocial services, as well as some who can manage with few or no services, have lost their relationship to anything that could meaningfully be called a home, while others in both categories have good linkages to family, a supportive community, and stable housing. In addition, the need for treatment and support varies across time and across many other dimensions (Ridgeway and Zipple, 1990, p. 23). A client population described as people whose relationship to home and community has been seriously damaged and who are unlikely to be able to recreate a sense of being "at home" by themselves will include those with a broad range of competence and ability as well as disability.

At times, supported housing staff may find that they are the social

support system for their clients—a role that can range from inappropri-
ate to impossible. If the provision of social support, in addition to
housing and access to mental health services, is accepted as the goal of a
supported housing program, it is clear that no sensible allocation of staff
time will ever be adequate to meet those needs. The full range of support,
for anyone, can be provided only in the context of a complex network of
relationships. This has important implications for designing the role of
staff. Staff should create access to community-based support, but they
cannot replace it.

If we are to plan programs coherently, two ways of talking (and
therefore thinking) in this field need to be challenged. Both are found in
a typical description of the goal of supported housing: to make "independent living in the community" possible.

First, independence is neither a possible nor a desirable goal. I
cannot provide for myself without the help of others, and I prefer not to
feel disappointed in myself because of that. In our work and social
relationships, we all need and offer many different types of support to
one another. We depend on family, friends, bank tellers, garbage collec-
tors, and the kindness of strangers. Our goal, personally and programmatically, should be functional *inter*dependence.

Second, "the" community should be defined realistically. In the
language of community mental health, "the" community most often
seems to refer to the residents of typical neighborhoods, although we
know that few tolerant, diverse, and supportive communities can be
found in the neighborhoods of our cities and towns. For long-term
intensive users of the mental health system, their friends, financial support, health, housing, and roommates are often tied to that system of
care. Except where family members have remained available, the only
dependable source of support may be other consumers and staff. The
mental health system may be the only significant community to which
they belong (Estroff, 1981, pp. 176–189).

One can be a member of many different types of community: the
community of mental health professionals, a neighborhood, a minority
group, an international community, and so on. Many people find a sense
of belonging within what has been called a *lifestyle enclave,* a group
composed of those who share one's interests and background (Bellah and
others, 1985, pp. 71–75; Fischer, 1982, pp.26–32).

There should not be a different standard for the psychiatrically
disabled. In fact, to describe successful living in "the" community only in
terms of relationships with nonclients is stigmatizing. It denies the value
of relationships with other clients. This does not mean that clients
should restrict their social network to other clients. It does mean that we
should equally value membership in that community.

Establishment of the Clustered Apartment Project

With help from a Robert Wood Johnson Foundation Mental Health Services Development grant, the Mental Health Bureau in Santa Clara County, California, created the Clustered Apartment Project. It is designed to provide a home and membership in a supportive community for those who lack that. Its clientele are those who formerly would have been tracked into residential treatment or other transitional programs. Ongoing funding for these programs comes from the transfer of resources from transitional residential programs (Mandiberg and Telles, 1990, pp. 22–23).

The initial conceptualization of this program model was the work of James Mandiberg and Thomas O'Brien, both formerly of the Santa Clara County Mental Health Bureau.

Housing

The programs within the Clustered Apartment Project deal with the economics of housing people who live on a disability income as many other supported housing programs do, by offering two or more clients of mental health services the option of sharing a house or an apartment. That can place a burden on relatively functional household members, if the less functional ones come to rely on them heavily. The problems this may create are similar to those experienced in families who care for a member who is psychiatrically disabled.

Furthermore, such living situations are often unstable no matter what the characteristics of the tenants are, not least because very little housing is properly designed for use by a group of unrelated adults (Martinez, 1990). Clients may be living in close quarters, for long periods of time, in housing that was originally designed for a multigenerational family. When single-bedroom, scattered-site housing is available, this can create the opposite problem. Tenants may become isolated, if they are unable to make the effort required to create a social network for themselves.

It is important not to pathologize these problems, or others such as those that result from living on a marginal income, by blaming them on the psychological characteristics of program clients. The design of a supported housing program should mitigate the generic problems involved in a housing situation before addressing any specific ones that may be the result of a person's disability. We have found that the creation of a supportive client-based community tends to compensate for the problems intrinsic to both single and shared housing. Membership in such a community provides escape from relationships that have become too intense and distributes the burden of support when one community member has overwhelming needs. It offers a social context, which is especially important for those who live alone.

At project sites we try to secure housing, for a 60- to 100-person community, within the boundaries of a neighborhood, so that members of the client community can get together easily to create a network of supportive relationships. Meeting rooms and a place that can be used for respite should also be located in that neighborhood. It is this intention that is responsible for calling this the Clustered Apartment Project. However, it may be only in dense urban areas that this much housing can be found within an easy walking distance without creating excessively high visibility. Where housing cannot be clustered, other ways must be found to create a sense of community membership. A recognition of the shared needs and interests of a community of clients is more fundamental to the Clustered Apartment Project model than is the physical clustering of program housing.

The Model and the Programs

The Clustered Apartment Project developed a conceptual model, not a program type. Project sites are unified by shared principles, not necessarily by shared practices. Each project site is similar in its intent to develop a stable client community on which members can rely for friendship and support. How it accomplishes that goal reflects the unique characteristics of each program's social and physical environment.

Current Project sites include the following:

1. The Community for Interdependent Living in San Jose, which houses sixty-eight people within an urban neighborhood. This is the only current site that has a housing display that fits the ideal of having a significant amount of program-controlled housing scattered within a single urban neighborhood. The proximity of this housing facilitated the rapid development of a strong sense of community at this site. Social events are easily accessible. An apartment within the cluster is kept available to be used as a client-operated respite center. If a problem develops, the community can be mobilized quickly for action or decision making.

2. In contrast, Community Alliance has seventy-three people in housing scattered throughout the suburbs of "Silicon Valley." The sense of community membership, while important to many members, is clearly more tenuous than at sites at which members are in regular face-to-face contact. Social events and meetings present formidable logistical problems.

To compensate, staff—the majority of whom are clients—have created additional ways to provide a sense of community to those who would otherwise be lost in the anonymity of the suburbs. A community newsletter serves as an effective forum for community contact and debate. Alternatives to "majority rules" voting are being developed to give a voice to the client community, since they cannot easily gather for discussion and decision making. The distance between housing has provided impetus to the development of effective mediation-based interventions to deal with intrahousehold conflict.

3. The Bridge Supported Housing Program houses ninety people in two adjacent small towns. Within each town, some clustering of housing and the use of bicycles make gatherings of community members relatively easy. Transportation is arranged when the whole community meets for social or decision-making events. A majority of both the staff and the clients are first- or second-generation Hispanic, so many have more life experience of strong community ties than do those at the other sites.

This site is also unique in providing access to treatment services, including twenty-four-hour staffed respite and medication prescription, within the parent agency. This has had a dramatic effect in reducing recidivism to low levels, relative to all other residential programs in the county, while simultaneously increasing the program's capacity to serve some of the most severely psychiatrically disabled of the county mental health system's clientele in ordinary shared-housing situations.

4. Casa Feliz is a sixty-bed single-room occupancy (SRO) hotel in downtown San Jose. Typically, SRO residents make it clear that they want to be left alone, so the application of the community development principles of the Clustered Apartment Project receives a severe test at such a site. While people like those who live in Casa Feliz may reject staff interventions and "house" rules, they also often share strong unstated ties and a clear value system, based on their life-style and interests. Those personal ties and values can be supported and reinforced.

Typical community-building processes were not effective at Casa Feliz. Few tenants will attend discussion and decision-making meetings. However, by relying on informal conversations in small groups, especially in relation to concrete and immediate issues, it has been possible to identify and respond to community wishes and to reinforce the need that these people, like others, have to belong to a supportive community.

Target Client Group

Admission to project sites is intended for people with a substantial history of psychiatric treatment who have been unable to maintain a social support system or stable housing. Applicants must be able to pay rent, which is typically set at one-third of income. There are no other rules or requirements.

The admission process is intended to discover whether the client community has the capacity to adapt to an applicant's needs, as opposed to an intake process that defines the characteristics successful applicants must possess. For example, if an applicant lacks certain "living" skills, admission depends on whether the members of the client community can provide a way to teach those skills or whether there is a household in which having those skills is not so important. There will be times when an applicant's needs will exceed the capacity of a project community to adapt, although in practice that has been rare.

Community

In the Clustered Apartment Project, clients are members of a community based in their housing. Social support is available within that community. The level of social interaction with others is determined by each community member for himself or herself. It can range from playing an active leadership role within the community to the mere fact of receiving a newsletter and being invited to community events. Participation is always invited, never required.

Anyone in a Clustered Apartment Project program who wishes to meet some or all of his or her social needs among people who have no connection with the mental health system will be helped to do so. These communities can operate as springboards from which members can move into other groups. However, the majority—those for whom, at least initially, that may be neither a possible nor a desirable goal—can find a dependable source of help, understanding, and friendship among others who share their background and concerns.

From the point of view of the Mental Health Bureau, as a funder, the membership of a client community at a project site is defined by the number of tenants living in program housing. This becomes the number of "units of service" provided under contract. However, over the years, each community has come to identify its membership as larger than that group of people who live in program housing. Some former tenants who have moved, current applicants not yet housed, and other clients in the area who may have their own housing but want access to client-based social support and acceptance may be members from the community's voice of view.

Staff

The staff role is the most difficult element of the Clustered Apartment Project to operationalize. We live in a culture that values independence (as mentioned, a senseless notion if taken literally and without context— independence from what?) over interdependence and that values the individual over the community. Even social work has come to mean the resolving of individual or family, rather than community, problems (Specht,

1990). In this atmosphere, our task has been to develop a staff group that has the ability to facilitate the creation of a supportive community.

Unlike clinicians and case managers who provide treatment-related services to individuals, the object of the work of these staff is the client community as a whole. One interesting consequence of this division of labor is that there is no justification for having program meetings or meeting places that are controlled by staff or closed to clients. Confidentiality and privacy are not an issue when the object of the staff's work is not what an individual needs but what a community wants.

We understand the need to provide good access to treatment and rehabilitation services, but it is critical to separate clearly the tasks of developing a supportive community from the provision of treatment or other services to individuals. This also applies to property management, which should be done by staff with a different job description than the ones who are community developers.

If a member in a project community is becoming isolated, the job of staff is to help that community find ways to maintain contact and provide support. If a situation is potentially dangerous, staff have the same obligations anyone else has, to aid a person in trouble, either by directly intervening or by getting help. In the early stages of community development, staff may have to be quite active in bringing support to those who need it. But the primary job the project staff is paid to do is to facilitate the development of dependable supportive relationships within the context of a client community.

The staff also need to ensure the development of appropriate organizational structures. For example, if complex issues are brought to regular community meetings for resolution, bad decisions are likely to result. Once again, this is unrelated to the nature of psychiatric disabilities. Bringing a complex issue to any diverse group and asking for a decision can have the same result. Staff should help the community develop focus groups or a think tank or other planning forums that can refine an issue until it is in a form that is appropriate to bring to a community's decision-making body.

Note that in this project, there is no staff-to-client ratio. There is a staff-to-community ratio. In one community with ninety members, there are three staff; at another with sixty-five members, there are four staff. More staff may be needed when there are large distances between houses, fewer when effective leadership has been developed within the community. In general, the larger the community, the less burden there is on staff because more, and more varied, abilities exist among its members.

Conflict Resolution

If, when there are conflicts between roommates or other program clients, it is staff who resolve the problem, the covert message is that clients are incompetent to manage their own affairs. In the Clustered Apartment Project, training in mediation techniques has been provided for members so that the resources for nonadversarial, peer-based dispute resolution are available within these communities.

The use of mediation has other benefits in addition to resolving disputes. In the process of training members to be mediators, the values built into this approach become embedded in the community as a whole. This includes trying to help everyone get what they want (rather than deciding who is right and who is wrong), understanding that the best decisions are usually the ones people make for themselves, and helping people realize that the problems they thought were unique to themselves are shared by others.

In most residential settings, the threat of eviction is the ultimate tool used to get clients to behave "properly" or in accordance with program rules. In a supported housing program, this is in direct conflict with the intent to provide stable housing, especially for those who historically have behaved in ways that caused them to lose their housing.

Whenever possible, unacceptable behavior should be seen as a problem to be resolved within the client community, keeping in mind that the person whose behavior is troubling is also a member of that community. Within a community context, a variety of sanctions other than eviction are possible. Supportive relationships can be offered as a reward or withheld as a punishment. Massed opinion, clearly expressed, can be very effective.

Community-based sanctions are a more powerful tool than most of us realize, because few of us are conscious of their role in our own lives. At the current stage of project development, eviction is rare, but even more could be done to create "win-win solutions" to disputes and, when sanctions are necessary, to make more effective use of the power of community membership.

Rights of Tenants Versus Funders

There is a dilemma at the heart of many mental health–funded housing programs. If, due to cost or other considerations, program clients must share housing, then:

1. If tenants have the right to reject prospective roommates, the funding source may be unable to house some of the people it wants to, in the housing for which it is paying.
2. If tenants do not have the right to reject prospective roommates, they may have to share their home with someone with whom they do not want to live. Even when current tenants have not participated in a "placement" decision, they may have to deal with the problem a new roommate creates in their home.

In the Clustered Apartment Project, housing choices are offered whenever possible, and current tenants have the right to refuse a reasonable number of prospective roommates before financial or other considerations take precedence over their wishes. When that does happen, it is important to renew the agreement by the client community to provide support to all households, if and when needed, and to treat an initial tenancy as an experiment. If there are irreconcilable differences within a household, those involved have the option of applying for other housing. At some sites, a special committee manages tenant movement within the program's stock of housing.

Current Design Issues

Currently, at all project sites, housing is seen as a resource to be used by a program to meet the needs of its clients. However, we are exploring the reconceptualization of housing as a community's "commons" (Berkes and Feeny, 1990), a collective resource to be managed (or even better, owned) by the community as a whole in the interest of meeting the need of its members for a home. At a Clustered Apartment Project site, community ownership would have some clear advantages over either program, household, or individual ownership of housing.

A related issue is that, in retrospect, instead of defining a client community in terms of tenancy in program-controlled housing, it might have been better if we had started by creating opportunities for all clients who live within a reasonable-size area to get together, and if we had defined the initial work of staff as the development of an awareness of shared interests within that group. Those interests would almost certainly include the need for social acceptance and for decent and affordable housing.

If that process resulted in developing housing to meet that need, the result might look similar to the outcomes of the Clustered Apartment Project, but this alternative approach would involve responding to needs that clients were helped to define for themselves, rather than ones that mental health program staff defined for them.

Working out these relationships between the boundaries of a client community and the housing needed by its members is the most recent example of our attempt to be consistent in the design of a program that has as its goal the creation of a home, in the context of a community, for those who need that.

The following standards were suggested by the Standards for Clubhouse Model programs (Fountain House, 1990). Collectively, these descriptions uniquely identify a program based on the Clustered Apartment Project model.

1. The client community is characterized by supportive relationships between its members.
2. Program housing is intended for people with a substantial history of psychiatric treatment who are unable to maintain adequate social supports or stable housing. Admission criteria are inclusive; that is, the community will attempt to adapt to an applicant's needs rather than defining the characteristics that successful applicants must possess.
3. Consistent but noncoercive contact is maintained with members who are not participating in community events or are otherwise becoming isolated. However, there are no contracts or rules intended to force participation by members.
4. Members participate in the work of the community, including intake and orientation, outreach, hiring and training of staff, advocacy, and program evaluation. The community makes maximum use of the collective knowledge, abilities, and skills of its members. The work that is done by members for the program is acknowledged and rewarded in a way that does not exploit them.
5. The information, skills, and abilities needed to organize, develop, and maintain a safe, supportive, and stable community exist within the staff group. Although staff carry overall responsibility for the state of the community, there are no specific tasks that can, or should, be done only by staff. (Specialized tasks—especially those related to property management, such as rent collection—and individual treatment and rehabilitation services should be provided by staff who are clearly distinguished from community development staff.)
6. Consistent efforts will be made by the program to ensure that staff jobs are accessible to members of the program community and other consumers of psychiatric services.
7. The program provides safe, decent, affordable housing for all community members, with no time limits on tenancy. Whenever possible, it offers a choice of type and location of housing. Tenancy can be maintained during an absence, including a hospitalization, by arranging for the payment of rent.
8. Ideally, program housing is dispersed within a neighborhood, with easy access to a central meeting place so that members can get together without depending on staff, and a sense of community identification develops easily. Where housing is separated by more than a comfortable walking distance, transportation must be available to community events and a special effort made to establish, for all members, a sense of belonging to the community.
9. All community meetings, where program decisions or individual members are discussed, and all community areas are accessible to all staff and members at all times.

10. A comprehensive orientation to the community—its structure, procedures, and values, as well as practical information intended to make new members feel at home and competent—is designed by staff and community members and provided to all its members.
11. The community is separate from institutional or other mental health settings, although all members have information about, and access to, treatment, rehabilitation, and advocacy services.
12. Conflict is addressed through community-based dispute resolution procedures—for example, mediation, implemented, whenever possible, by trained members of the client community.
13. The community provides support and encouragement to members who are attempting to secure, sustain, or upgrade their opportunities for employment and education, or who are maintaining relationships with friends and family outside the client community.
14. Members who are employed or at school continue to have access to the social support of the community and have input into community decisions.
15. Community members participate in all internal decision-making processes that affect the operation and functioning of the community. The community as a whole takes responsibility for setting its own goals and evaluating its effectiveness in meeting those goals.
16. The community maintains a process through which it is able to advise relevant decision-making bodies on issues that affect it, including the development of its budget.

Epilogue

One project site offers respite for any community member who wants that, in an apartment called the Center of Attention. One evening I attended a meeting of the members who volunteer to stay in this apartment when needed. They were working out schedules. After the meeting, the woman whose turn it was to stay there left to get what she needed for the night. I was talking with a staff member on the sidewalk outside when she returned.

She crossed the park that separated her apartment from the one used for respite. I could see her toothbrush sticking out of the paper sack she carried. What I remember most clearly is how she walked. She was not a "crisis worker" rushing back to aid others in need. She was just on her way to help her neighbors.

References

Bellah, R. N., Madsen, R., Sullivan, W. M., Swidler, A., and Tipton, S. M. *Habits of the Heart: Individualism and Commitment in American Life*. Berkeley: University of California Press, 1985.

Berkes, F., and Feeny, D. "Paradigms Lost." *Alternatives,* 1990, *17* (2), 48–55.

Cooper, R. "Dwelling and the Therapeutic Community." In R. Cooper (ed.), *Thresholds Between Philosophy and Psychoanalysis.* London: Free Association Books, 1989.

Estroff, S. *Making It Crazy.* Berkeley: University of California Press, 1981.

Fischer, C. *To Dwell Among Friends.* Chicago: University of Chicago Press, 1982.

Fountain House, Inc. "Standards for Clubhouse Model Programs." Unpublished manuscript, Fountain House, Inc., New York, 1990.

Mandiberg, J., and Telles, L. "The Santa Clara County Clustered Apartment Project." *Psychosocial Rehabilitation Journal,* 1990, *14* (2), 22–23.

Martinez, E. "What Makes Group Housing Work: Architectural Design Guidelines for New Facilities." Unpublished manuscript, Eduardo Martinez Design Associates, San Francisco, 1990.

Ridgeway, P., and Zipple, A. M. "The Paradigm Shift in Residential Services." *Psychosocial Rehabilitation Journal,* 1990, *13* (4), 11–30.

Specht, H. "Social Work and the Popular Psychotherapies." *Social Service Review,* 1990, *64* (3), 345–357.

LAWRENCE TELLES is director of the Cluster Apartment Project, Santa Clara County, San Jose, California.

Led by Northern Rhode Island Community Mental Health Center's demonstration program, Rhode Island's mobile treatment teams for persons with mental illness, substance abuse, and legal problems are altering service delivery approaches statewide.

Treating Persons with Mental Illness, Substance Abuse, and Legal Problems: The Rhode Island Experience

Ann Detrick, Virginia Stiepock

Rhode Island is reshaping its mental health system to better meet the needs of persons too often labeled as difficult to serve—that is, young adults who suffer the multiple effects of mental illness, substance abuse, and legal problems. In this chapter, we will describe how the statewide development of self-contained service units, known as *mobile treatment teams* (MTTs), is sparking renewed staff commitment and service innovation on behalf of these persons. We will review the service delivery values and skills developed by Rhode Island's initial demonstration MTT, operated by the Northern Rhode Island Community Mental Health Center (NRI).

Northern Rhode Island's demonstration MTT has given priority to serving young adults whose psychiatric, substance abuse, and legal difficulties have resulted in repeated involuntary state hospital and medical detoxification admissions, frequent periods of homelessness, recurring contacts with the police, and ongoing poverty. NRI's MTT operates seven days per week, including evenings and holidays. It provides outreach via telephone and home visits, crisis intervention, and intensive case management in the form of daily contacts with clients in their homes or other community settings (for example, police stations, courtrooms, and homeless shelters). In contrast to the traditional linkage model of case management, the goal of the NRI MTT is to serve as the fixed point of responsibility for addressing clients' needs in a range of areas including psychiatric, housing, vocational, substance abuse, and legal involvement. Other features of the NRI MTT include solid teamwork by multidisciplinary staff, small client-to-staff ratio, and relationship building with consumers. Because many MTT clients have tended to disaffiliate from established mental health services, the demonstration MTT has emphasized the importance of blending practical and clinical supports within a context of consumer choice and self-determination.

NRI's demonstration program is leading the development of MTT programs across the state and altering the direction of Rhode Island's community mental health system. To set a context for this statewide change effort, we will begin with an overview of the current mental health system in Rhode Island.

Rhode Island's Mental Health System

Over the past decade, Rhode Island's mental health system has been successful in dramatically reducing its dependence on institutionalized care for persons with severe and persistent mental illness. Simultaneously, the state has developed an extensive system of community-based care built on a statewide structure of eight community mental health centers, augmented by several specialty agencies.

Rhode Island, the smallest state geographically, measures 1,200 square miles with a total population of approximately one million. Presently, nearly 5,500 persons with severe and persistent mental illness are served annually in Rhode Island's public mental health system. The single state-operated psychiatric patient facility, the Institute of Mental Health, has 194 licensed beds, including a twenty-bed forensic unit. The average daily census for fiscal year 1991 was 142. Because of recent changes within Rhode Island's mental health system, the Institute of Mental Health now serves primarily as a long-term treatment and rehabilitation facility. Since 1990, the Department of Mental Health, Retardation, and Hospitals (MHRH) has contracted with Butler Hospital, a Brown University–affiliated private psychiatric hospital, as the state's major provider of acute psychiatric services. General hospital acute psychiatric inpatient beds are also utilized by the community mental health centers.

The successful development of a community-based mental health system in Rhode Island can be tied to several factors.

MHRH has consistently articulated a singular mission that identifies community services for persons with severe and persistent mental illness as the highest service priority. Rhode Island's Comprehensive Mental Health Plan (1988), which formally embraces this mission, was developed through the active participation of key representatives within the system, including clients, family members, service providers, the General Assembly, and the governor. The Rhode Island community mental health system has a coherent, visible structure. One community mental health center in each of eight catchment areas is responsible for the entry of clients into the system and the delivery of an array of mental health services. With well-defined and accessible entry points as well as clear identification of responsibility, service fragmentation and accountability issues are generally absent.

One authority within MHRH has historically controlled funding for both state hospital and community services. This funding mechanism has permitted the ongoing transfer of monies from state hospital to community. MHRH has enhanced this movement of funds from institutional settings by creating financial incentives for mental health providers to effectively serve clients in the community.

Despite the achievements of Rhode Island's mental health system, significant service gaps have remained. As elsewhere, one of the most serious gaps has been the availability of adequate outreach, treatment, and support services for young adults who have been reluctant to involve themselves with, or have not responded to, existing community-based services. These young persons generally suffer from both mental illness and substance abuse, with many facing the additional complication of legal involvement. There is increasing recognition of the problem of substance use and abuse among young persons with mental illness (Drake and Wallach, 1989; Ridgely, Goldman, and Talbott, 1986). The relatively high incidence of legal contacts for these dually diagnosed young persons has also been substantiated (Holcomb and Ahr, 1988; McFarland and others, 1989).

Rhode Island's Comprehensive Mental Health Plan (1988) indicates that at least 447 young adults statewide require specialized, intensive treatment and support services for mental illness, substance abuse, and legal problems. This need has persisted despite the presence of well-established, catchment area–based case management programs. Traditionally, these programs have relied heavily on an individual case manager model, with staff providing direct care in addition to service brokerage. Each case manager carries a caseload of twenty to thirty. These case management services have worked well for many clients, with most programs having impressively low dropout rates.

The case management programs have been less successful in engaging young adults with multiple service needs. This has generally been due to the programs' moderate to high caseloads, lack of extensive outreach services, minimal evening and weekend coverage, and limited resources to address clients' substance abuse and legal issues. Other mental health center services (for example, residential, day treatment, vocational) have also had difficulty engaging these young persons, in part because of their requirements for regular client participation in structured, facility-based programs.

Statewide Mobile Treatment Team Initiative

In 1988, MHRH sought to create more responsive ways to serve young adults with mental illness, substance abuse, and legal problems. With support from the Robert Wood Johnson Foundation's Mental Health Ser-

vice Development Program, MHRH planned for the statewide establishment of continuous treatment teams or MTTs. These MTT services were
patterned on the Training in Community Living model developed in
Dane County, Wisconsin (Stein and Test, 1978, 1982).

Fashioned to address the limitations of existing mental health services, each MTT was to be a self-contained service unit, incorporating the
following features: (1) extensive outreach, (2) integration of treatment,
rehabilitation, and support services delivered primarily in settings outside of mental health center offices; (3) heavy emphasis on staff teamwork; (4) favorable client-to-staff ratio (no more than eight to one); (5)
extended service hours, including evenings and weekends; and (6) long-
term commitment to clients as long as their needs persist. Additionally,
each team was to incorporate emerging dual-diagnosis treatment approaches (Osher and Kofoed, 1989; Pepper and Ryglewicz, 1986; Sciacca,
1987) and initiate a variety of criminal justice contacts and interventions
on behalf of clients.

Northern Rhode Island's Demonstration Program

To launch the statewide effort, MHRH worked with two community
mental health centers to establish an initial, cross–catchment area demonstration MTT program. Adopting the continuous treatment team approach outlined above, NRI, the host agency, started an MTT program
designed to serve up to sixty-five young adults who (1) are aged eighteen
to forty; (2) in addition to a primary diagnosis of major mental illness,
have a primary or secondary diagnosis of a substance use disorder,
according to criteria set forth in DSM-III-R; (3) have current or past
involvement with the criminal justice system or are known to local
authorities as being at risk for criminal offenses; and (4) in order to
remain engaged in services, are assessed to need a more intensive level of
outreach and treatment than can be provided through existing community mental health services.

By establishing the NRI demonstration MTT program, MHRH sought
to develop and refine a set of service delivery values and skills that would
lead to MTT program development statewide.

Setting. Before implementation of the NRI MTT, many of the young
persons who eventually would be referred to the new program were
marginally connected to their families, friends, and the mental health
system. No mental health center program had been effective in helping
these young adults achieve stability in their lives. NRI's clinically focused
case management program was strong, with persistent outreach services
and few dropouts. Still, a number of young persons with very disabling
psychiatric conditions had only intermittent crisis contacts with NRI.
Frequently, the crises involved the police.

As NRI struggled to develop effective services for these young persons, their common characteristics were identified: severe and persistent mental illness substance disorder, and criminal justice involvement (or risk). In the past, no single agency had claimed responsibility for addressing the needs of this group. Clinically, the treatment picture was complicated by the overlap of symptoms and behaviors. The fact that symptoms were not easily or quickly differentiated and that one individual might have three or more diagnoses according to DSM-III-R had not changed treatment approaches. To effectively serve these young adults, a more integrated service model was required.

A "consumer-friendly" approach was called for, since existing services were not attractive to potential service recipients. While these young adults had difficulty managing their lives in the community, they did not routinely seek help. Mental health interventions were generally viewed as controlling and stigmatizing. Despite formidable personal obstacles, these young persons were often resourceful and tenacious in their efforts to sustain a normal community life.

Once staff began to understand some of the reasons for the young adults' persistence in refusing services, NRI was able to shift the focus of service delivery. Rather than continue to react to these young persons simply during crises, the agency began to lay a framework for establishing trusting long-term relationships with them. Forging these alliances required, first and foremost, that staff respect clients' desire to live apart from organized service systems or institutions. With this approach as the foundation, NRI began an integrated MTT service designed to reach out to clients and help them to manage their mental illness, substance abuse, and legal problems.

Program Start. NRI developed an MTT comprised of two master's and six bachelor's case managers, a nurse, and a part-time psychiatrist. Staff with expertise in mental health or substance abuse or both were recruited. Continuous treatment team elements were introduced, including integration of multiple services within one program entity, emphasis on staff teamwork, extended service hours, and small client-to-staff ratio (no more than eight to one). Referrals to the team were phased in gradually to facilitate relationship building with both consumers and community contacts (such as police, judges, and homeless shelter staff).

At the MTT's start, a program evaluation mechanism was established to clarify program goals, set expectations for staff performance, and assess service outcomes. Permanent housing and stable employment were primary client-based objectives along with the reduction of substance abuse, acute psychiatric symptoms, arrests, and affiliated functional impairments. Quality of life was expected to improve with stability of basic living conditions and enhancement of personal options.

These were well-intentioned objectives, but they could be achieved only if the MTT services were meaningful to each consumer's personal needs, interests, and life-style. Accordingly, the following service delivery guidelines were accentuated:

Maintain continuous, ongoing contact with the client, even through family and friends, when necessary
Maintain and enhance clients' integration with their community and natural support system, including family and peers
Foster collaboration with families, landlords, police, judges, employers, and other involved parties
Expect motivation to be the responsibility of the provider, not the client
Encourage abstinence, but do not make it a precondition for services
Divert from institutions, including psychiatric hospitals, detoxification units, jails and prisons
Help clients to understand the effects of their mental illness and substance abuse and gain effective control over their lives
Review outcome data as the program unfolds.

Operations. With the program objectives and service delivery guidelines in place, the MTT began operations. One of the most critical features of the program has been the integration of multiple services, provided through *ensemble* teamwork. In this approach, all MTT staff share responsibility for addressing each client's comprehensive treatment, rehabilitation, and support needs. While one primary case manager is assigned to each client, all MTT staff members work on the client's behalf. Occasionally, some tasks are assumed by virtue of a staff person's specialty area or skill level (such as nursing or psychiatry), while other more generic services are routinely shared by all staff (for example, counseling or symptom management).

With all MTT staff involved in clients' lives, there is consistent service delivery seven days a week. The team approach also diffuses the intensity of the relationship for clients and staff and lessens the impact when there is staff turnover. Most important for the young adults served, the unified team effort has minimized the service fragmentation that too often characterized their past contacts with the mental health, substance abuse, and criminal justice systems.

The overall success of MTT teamwork has hinged on careful staff communication and planning. MTT staff attend daily team meetings during which each client's status is reviewed and interventions are scheduled. Extensive assessment of client needs and regular treatment planning sessions have also been essential. Assessments and treatment plans are used as working documents that drive specific, individualized interventions for each client.

The benefits of an integrated team approach were quickly accepted by staff, but the day-to-day operation was not easily accomplished. A few original staff were unable to adapt to working primarily on street corners and in other community settings, such as police stations or homeless shelters. Some staff had trouble shedding well-established professional ideologies. For example, several staff with substance abuse expertise, trained according to a strict abstinence model, could not adjust to the team's less restrictive approach.

Staff who finally formed the core of the MTT program were committed to its service philosophy and team approach. Combining skill, flexibility, and sensitivity to client needs and interests, the staff have come to understand when traditional interventions are called for or when innovation may be in order.

Interventions. A wide range of interventions are seen as crucial.

Relationship Building. As the program began, relationship building with clients was one of the greatest challenges. Emergencies were often the first connecting point, offering an immediate opportunity for staff to show advocacy and support. As contact increased, it became clear that clients needed ongoing, daily support and structure to manage their lives.

Through intensive outreach and establishment of trusting relationships, staff have sought to help clients articulate the discomfort and life consequences of their psychiatric, substance abuse, and legal problems. Through this awareness, which is ongoing, clients and staff have worked together to negotiate the addition of structures and supports designed to alleviate life distress. Daily medication deliveries, a representative payee system, several program-leased apartments, and probation-mandated treatment are among the interventions that have eased the disorder in clients' lives. These structures have not only hastened personal successes but have also created a framework on which clients can build long-term goals.

Liaison/Collaboration with Community Contacts and Families. Building relationships with community members (such as families, general hospital emergency room staff, police, judges, and landlords) has been as important as relationship building with clients. Initial connections with the community swiftly led to active collaboration and shared problem solving, as police, judges, and other community members took notice of staff's follow-through on difficult issues. Families have played an invaluable role, serving as steady contact points for program staff and active participants in assessment and treatment planning.

Housing. Helping clients to achieve more stable housing arrangements has been a priority for MTT staff. Many clients entered the program with reputations as "poor housing risks." Some had been repeatedly rejected from existing mental health residential programs. Others were known to private landlords who refused to rent to them.

Since their involvement with the MTT program, many clients' housing problems have been solved by proactive, practical MTT staff interventions. Through outreach with both clients and landlords, staff have been able to anticipate problems and find creative solutions. Staff have accompanied clients to apply for income subsidies, helped them clean their apartments prior to inspections, or called landlords "just to hear how things are going."

More structured interventions have been used for a small number of clients with no income source, extremely poor rental histories, or unproven ability to live on their own without close staff supervision. For these individuals, the NRI administration rented two apartments, with MTT staff helping clients move into them, on an "as-needed" basis. Identified as the "transitional apartments," these living situations have provided flexible, supported housing arrangements and given a number of clients their first housing success.

Representative Payee System. Housing stability is closely linked with financial stability. One of the most serious consequences of clients' mental illness and substance abuse problems is difficulty managing limited financial resources. When this issue constitutes a threat to basic housing, food, and other life necessities, NRI acts as representative payee for clients. An administrative assistant disburses money to clients at scheduled times according to budgets negotiated between clients and staff. Aiding clients in regulating spending has promoted increased stability and self-control.

Psychiatric Symptom Management. Staff talk frequently with clients about their psychiatric symptoms and discuss how symptoms are interfering with daily life activity. Staff help clients develop methods that may lessen the symptoms' effects. Overall, while staff acknowledge that clients have a mental illness, they work to prevent the illness from becoming life defining. By offering coping strategies to ease the stresses of daily life, staff actively work with consumers to open avenues to normal community life. The ongoing collaboration of the team's psychiatrist with both clients and staff has been essential.

Substance Abuse Treatment. A nonconfrontational, educational approach has characterized the team's substance abuse interventions. Similar to the individual one-to-one psychiatric symptom contacts, staff have worked to help clients see the day-to-day consequences of their substance use. Staff have assisted individual clients in recognizing the relationship between their mental illness and substance use, as well as the interaction of substances with psychotropic medications. When clients begin to acknowledge problem areas, staff help them find ways to minimize or eliminate substance abuse. This has included offsetting their often endless, unstructured days with positive leisure time, or in some cases, employment. Group substance abuse treatment has been part of the team's work, with staff attending AA or NA meetings with individual clients or leading an in-house substance abuse group, which eight to ten MTT consumers generally attend. The team's nontraditional substance abuse treatment for its dually diagnosed clients has reduced, and in a few cases eliminated, the incidence of substance use.

Legal Advocacy/Negotiation. MTT staff have become excellent consumer advocates, but when a person with serious mental illness is actively abusing substances, the staff's role as advocate becomes less clear. Add criminal charges, and the picture becomes muddled. Staff often struggle with issues of accountability and enabling. Are clients accountable for criminal behaviors when psychotic or intoxicated? What is the staff's role under these circumstances? Will advocacy on the part of staff enable continued criminal or self-destructive behavior?

To assist the staff in applying specific types of advocacy, a team planning process occurs for each individual facing criminal charges. Through this process, the following questions are asked: Do criminal behaviors occur only during periods of decompensation or substance abuse? How does the client's substance abuse relate to his or her subjective experience of mental illness? In nearly all MTT cases, staff have assessed clients' criminal involvement to be tied to their mental illness or substance use or both and have recommended treatment alternatives in lieu of incarceration.

For clients who face criminal charges, staff play an active role, accompanying them to court, providing education as needed about the charges and court processes, and lobbying for adequate legal representation. Staff have also established high visibility with judges, probation officers, and other court personnel, educating them about the client's mental illness and substance abuse and, when warranted, recommending treatment alternatives to incarceration. Police, judges, and probation officers have been particularly responsive to MTT staff recommendations, often expressing relief that clients' mental illness and substance abuse problems are finally being addressed.

The goal of the MTT program is to prevent clients from committing criminal acts and risking incarceration. However, when the effects of a client's mental illness or substance abuse lead to a criminal charge, the MTT staff often choose to work within the criminal justice system to leverage engagement in treatment. MTT staff frequently recommend probation-ordered treatment for clients facing charges, and police and judges have been receptive to this intervention. While this approach results in both criminal justice and mental health staff imposing external controls over clients' lives, the conditions of probation are actively negotiated among the client, MTT staff, and probation officer. Since most clients have had repeated contacts with the criminal justice system, often in the absence of advocacy and support, they are generally willing to agree to work cooperatively with MTT staff to avoid further criminal sanctions.

Case Example. The following case summary illustrates how team interventions have been used to engage clients in treatment and promote positive outcomes.

Prior to MTT involvement, Mary, thirty-one years old, turned to NRI as a last resort, long after the voices had taken over. When she needed drug money, she turned to the streets, where she was often badly abused. NRI had attempted outreach, but she did not maintain ongoing contact.

After one of Mary's arrests for prostitution, police called NRI to report that she was out of control and psychotic. There were new track marks on her arm. Emergency services staff first arranged for Mary to go to an involuntary medical detoxification unit, from which she was transferred on a ten-day commitment to a local general hospital psychiatric unit. MTT staff were introduced to Mary on the psychiatric unit and then attempted numerous outreach contacts when she left the hospital and returned to her room in a local boardinghouse.

During the first six months, MTT contact with Mary was sporadic. She often declined to talk to staff when they knocked on her door or approached her on a local street corner. She rejected psychiatric medication and continued to abuse street drugs. When she was evicted from her room for nonpayment of rent and destruction of property, staff lost contact with Mary for months. They searched for her in local bars and homeless shelters, but it was through her sister that staff found her— living with an old boyfriend. Staff resumed contact with Mary but placed no demands on her in an effort to build trust. In a few months, she needed to find another place to live.

With no money, Mary accepted staff's suggestion that she move to the transitional apartment for a while "to get back on her feet." After a few weeks at the apartment, Mary agreed to take lithium, which the staff brought to her daily. As she began to feel better, she accepted a staff person's offer to take her to the YMCA for classes. With a stable living situation, medication, and added structure to her days, Mary's use of street drugs dropped. She still used alcohol, but not as frequently. After she had lived in the transitional apartment for three months, staff helped her find an apartment she could afford.

The MTT program has served Mary for two years. The program assists her with budgeting, which ensures there is enough money for rent. Since taking lithium, she has not had police contact. In talking with Mary and reviewing her history (through family contacts and agency records), staff have determined that her arrests for prostitution were tied to manic episodes. Mary continues with little street drug use, but her abuse of alcohol has not stopped. Within the last few months, she has had two voluntary medical detoxification admissions, and she attends AA meetings several times a week with an MTT staff person. Mary occasionally finds part-time work on her own, and staff are looking at ways to help her establish steady employment.

Program Outcomes

The goal of the program evaluation component has been to compare each client's status on six variables, before and after involvement with the MTT. The six variables are psychiatric hospital admission, admission to medical detoxification units, arrests, emergency services contacts, housing changes, and employment. The first eighteen-month follow-up study, which was conducted on the initial seventeen clients in the program, shows reductions in the incidence of psychiatric hospitalization, detoxification admissions, emergency services contacts, and arrests. There were no reductions in the number of housing changes during the eighteen-month post-MTT versus pre-MTT period. The first eighteen-month follow-up data also show no gains in client employment status.

While post-MTT data for subsequent follow-up periods await final analyses, initial trends indicate that clients continue to have reduced psychiatric hospital and detoxification admissions. When psychiatric hospital or detoxification admissions occur, they are generally voluntary in nature, indicating clients' recognition of the effects of their symptoms and willingness to accept treatment before their problems become severe. While few clients have achieved abstinence, most have substantially reduced their use of one or more substances. Police contacts have also dropped. Frequency of housing changes has declined, indicating that staff's initial efforts to facilitate stable housing are beginning to pay off. Particularly impressive to staff has been the low client dropout rate. Since the program's inception, only two clients, both of whom were stable in treatment, have asked to leave the program. One of them subsequently returned to NRI for services, at his request.

The employment results to date are disappointing. Thirteen of the original seventeen clients were employed during the eighteen-month follow-up period, compared with twelve clients employed prior to MTT contact. Stable employment was achieved by a few clients during their involvement with the MTT program (for example, five gained full-time employment during the first eighteen months, with two persons having more than one full year of employment). Most clients who became employed while with the MTT held part-time jobs of short duration.

There may be several explanations for the lack of progress in the area of employment. Given the many difficulties that clients were experiencing prior to MTT program involvement, initial staff activities focused primarily on clinical and behavioral issues affecting housing and personal stability. Staff turnover in the early phases of the program may have been a factor, since during times of personnel changes, highest priority was assigned to maintaining clients' basic life needs. The unfavorable economic climate has not been helpful. Traditional attitudes about mentally ill clients' capacity to work, as well as MTT staff's limited knowledge of job development and support techniques, may also represent significant obstacles. It is interesting that most of the original seventeen MTT clients had employment experience prior to involvement with the program. This is a testament to the resilience and strength of these young clients, whose lives have been so disrupted by mental illness, substance abuse, and legal trouble. Given the financial and personal benefits that work can bring to this young consumer group, Rhode Island needs to take additional steps to ensure that employment services become an integral part of MTT programs.

Several outcomes were not anticipated. The program has found that individuals with mood disorders often have difficulty relating to a treatment team and experience better outcomes when assigned primarily to one staff. For several clients with mood disorders, the program has accommodated their preference and arranged primarily one-to-one work. Programmatically, during the course of the NRI MTT demonstration, a total of fifty consumers have been served. The original caseload target was sixty-five. Several factors may be responsible for the lower-than-expected utilization rate. Given the comprehensive community mental health system and extensive outreach programs already in place in the two catchment areas, only the most unreachable clients were known at the start of the program. Also, as a result of staff turnover at the program's beginning, case finding activities were temporarily curtailed. In addition, the program's eligibility criteria have been strict, requiring that clients be under forty years of age and have mental health, substance abuse, and legal issues. As the project evolved, the age eligibility criterion was increased from forty to forty-five, but this has not resulted in a significant increase in referral.

It may be fortuitous that the caseload has not reached sixty-five, since the program has felt stretched to respond adequately to the needs of fifty consumers. While MHRH is presently developing service guidelines for other MTT programs around the state, the current assessment is that a six-to-one client-to-staff ratio (caseload of fifty-four for nine full-time staff) may be appropriate for a seasoned MTT program serving this high-need consumer group.

Conclusion

Since the start of Rhode Island's MTT initiative three years ago, seven MTT programs have been developed statewide. More than 300 young adults with intensive treatment and support needs are now benefiting from these services. The staff dedication and service technology of the NRI demonstration program have captured the attention of mental health advocates and providers throughout Rhode Island. Dual-diagnosis curriculum training and conferences have been held, and each of the eight community mental health centers is now licensed as a dual-diagnosis treatment provider. MHRH is disseminating statewide MTT standards that define the necessary ingredients of the integrated, team-based service delivery approach.

Overall, the seven MTT programs are rekindling the state's long-standing commitment to community mental health care. Most important, each local MTT program is inspiring a grass-roots shift in values. Within each mental health center catchment area, administrators, staff, and advocates are taking a fresh look at existing program models and making changes directed toward more individualized, consumer-driven services.

References

Drake, R. E., and Wallach, M. A. "Substance Abuse Among the Chronic Mentally Ill." *Hospital and Community Psychiatry,* 1989, *40* (10), 1041–1045.

Holcomb, W. R., and Ahr, P. R. "Arrest Rates Among Young Adult Psychiatric Patients Treated in Inpatient and Outpatient Settings." *Hospital and Community Psychiatry,* 1988, *39* (1), 52–57.

McFarland, B. H., Faulkner, L. R., Bloom, J. D., Hallaux, R., and Bray, J. D. "Chronic Mental Illness and the Criminal Justice System." *Hospital and Community Psychiatry,* 1989, *40* (7), 718–723.

Osher, F. C., and Kofoed, L. L. "Treatment of Patients with Psychiatric and Psychoactive Substance Abuse Disorders." *Hospital and Community Psychiatry,* 1989, *40* (10), 1025–1029.

Pepper, B., and Ryglewicz, H. "Guidelines for Treating the Young Adult Chronic Patient." *TIE Lines,* 1986, *3* (1), 1–8.

Rhode Island Department of Mental Health, Retardation, and Hospitals. *Decade of Progress: Rhode Island State Mental Health Plan, 1989–1998.* Providence: Rhode Island Department of Mental Health, Retardation, and Hospitals, 1988.

Ridgely, M. S., Goldman, H. H., and Talbott, J. A. *Chronic Mentally Ill Young Adults with Substance Abuse Problems: A Review of Relevant Literature and Creation of a Research Agenda.* Baltimore: Mental Health Policy Studies, Department of Psychiatry, School of Medicine, University of Maryland, 1986.

Sciacca, K. "New Initiatives in the Treatment of the Chronic Patient with Alcohol/Substance Use Problems." *TIE Lines,* 1987, *4* (3), 5–6.

Stein, L., and Test, M. A. "An Alternative to Mental-Hospital Treatment." In L. Stein and M. A. Test (eds.), *An Alternative to Mental Hospital Treatment.* New York: Plenum, 1978.

Stein, L., and Test, M. A. "Community Treatment of the Young Adult Patient." In B. Pepper and H. Ryglewicz (eds.), *The Young Adult Chronic Patient.* New Directions for Mental Health Services, no. 4. San Francisco: Jossey-Bass, 1982.

ANN DETRICK *is statewide project development director of Rhode Island's mobile treatment team initiative. She works in the Division of Mental Health and Management Services, Office of Community Support Services.*

VIRGINIA STIEPOCK *is assistant center director/clinical director of the Northern Rhode Island Community Mental Health Center, Inc.*

A system of care for seriously mentally ill older adults incorporates concepts from programs for healthy older adults and challenges traditional concepts of mental health treatment.

An Innovative Program for Community-Residing Older Adults with Serious Mental Illness

Marla Hassinger Martin, Bernice Bratter

This chapter highlights the Community Connections Project, a program of innovative services for the seriously mentally ill elderly, funded as a three-year demonstration project by the Robert Wood Johnson Foundation. Since its inception in 1988, the project has served over 160 acutely or persistently mentally ill older adults each year. The project site, Senior Health and Peer Counseling in Santa Monica, California, has a fourteen-year history of providing innovative interdisciplinary health care services to older adults residing in the Westside of Los Angeles County.

In the sections that follow, we will introduce a philosophy of community-based mental health care derived from Senior Health and Peer Counseling's perspective and philosophy, address the need for services for seriously mentally ill older adults, and describe how the Community Connections Project uses formal and informal community supports to optimize the capacity of older people to function at reasonable levels of health and well-being.

The Setting

Senior Health and Peer Counseling is a private, nonprofit organization founded in 1976 in response to a lack of affordable health care for older citizens. The Westside of Los Angeles County has a percentage of older people that is approximately twice the national average and that is growing rapidly. The majority of the services provided at the agency are not available through other public or private sources. Fees for services are on a sliding scale, according to an individual's ability to pay, and over 75 percent of clients are low income.

Programs focus on prevention of disease, education for a healthy life-style, and assistance with the special emotional concerns that aging brings. The complex health needs of older people are addressed through an interdisciplinary approach that takes into account the whole person—physical, emotional, and social. The use of volunteers is a hallmark of the agency's approach. It enables services to be extremely cost effective and adds a dimension of service that is enriching.

Senior Health and Peer Counseling offers several unique features that act as catalysts for success in serving the seriously mentally ill elderly. Providing services in a community-based interdisciplinary health care agency, as differentiated from a traditional mental health facility, creates a nonthreatening environment. People who come for services see active, healthy older adults participating as employees, as volunteers, as students, and as clients. Thus, the model diminishes the stigma so often attached to mental illness and traditional mental health facilities. Because of its philosophy of training and utilizing older adults as volunteers, the organization has received national attention, including exposure on *60 Minutes* and *20/20* and designation as one of President Bush's "Points of Light."

Evolution of the Community Connections Project

The project has evolved in response to a wide range of needs.

Local Need. Santa Monica, California, has an unusually high proportion of older adults. In 1985, 27 percent of its population was age fifty-five or older, and the area had no public mental health services offered by specialists in gerontology or geriatrics. Additionally, more and more older adults with serious mental illness were being seen on the streets and at the agency, partially in response to a countywide funding crisis that resulted in the cutback of many mental health services in the mid 1980s. A revolving-door situation evolved in which there were less-than-adequate services to support people in the community and in which brief hospitalizations seemed to be the only treatment available for decompensating clients. While Senior Health and Peer Counseling was not staffed to serve this population in 1985, its overall concept has made the agency an ideal organization for developing a successful, well-utilized program that could offer services not otherwise available.

National Need. In addition to the community's particular situation, several other factors prompted Senior Health and Peer Counseling to invest in serving the chronically mentally ill senior. Older adults have a high prevalence of psychiatric problems, because of age-related changes (Srole and others, 1962; Kramer, Tauge, and Redick, 1973) such as increased physical illness, isolation and losses of social support, inadequate finances, and the association between age and organic mental disorders (Butler and Lewis, 1982). Completed suicides among the elderly are disproportionately high, rising at succeeding age levels to a rate of 51.4 per 100,000 for white men age eighty to eighty-four (Pfeiffer, 1977). Even so, utilization of mental health services by older adults is lower than for any other age group except children (Zarit, 1980).

In California, older adults (age sixty plus) are grossly underfunded and underserved by mental health programs; although they represent 16 percent of the population, older adults received only 4 to 6 percent of mental health services, and it is estimated that 80 percent of older adults needing mental health services are not served by existing programs (Acosta, Cohen, Green, and Wulke, 1991).

One of the major system problems affecting older adults' use of mental health resources is that the community mental health movement of the 1960s and the resulting mental health programs took shape with younger populations in mind; planning did not adequately address the needs of older adults.

Although older adults across the country are underserved now with respect to mental health, long-range projections indicate an even worse state of crisis if planners do not respond to demographic projections that tell us of the aging of our population, both with respect to average life expectancy and to the overall percentage of older adults in the population (Atchley, 1985). According to U.S. Census figures, people sixty-five years of age and over currently number about 20.4 million. By the year 2030, this number will increase to 64.8 million. The fastest-growing segment of the elderly population, those age eighty-five and older, will be particularly vulnerable.

Barriers to Access. Why is mental health service utilization so sparse and inadequate? Unfortunately, many health care providers and older adults themselves foster the bias that older adults are not capable of benefiting from traditional treatments of choice for younger adults. Psychotherapy is a case in point. Although there has been a movement to dispel this myth, exemplified in Whelihan (1979), much work and advocacy must be done before service providers become enthusiastic about serving older adults.

Several other important barriers to access are addressed by Curian (1982). Government regulations, for example, still encourage institutional care rather than community care by restricting outpatient mental health care benefits. Psychological impediments to access include, for instance, asking minority seniors to trust "the establishment's" representatives, or expecting a cohort of adults not raised in an atmosphere of psychological-mindedness to seek out mental health services. Other more concrete access problems include transportation problems and need for outreach to homebound people.

It is clear that there is a great need to develop services in response to the mental health needs of older adults. We share the opinion of Senator John Melcher (1988, p. 643) that "we need to switch the focus of our public assistance for health care away from institutional care and toward home and community-based medical and social services for elderly Americans. Both financial and humanitarian considerations point to this conclusion."

The Community Connections Project validated the impact of both traditional and innovative services in enhancing the quality of lives as well as the self-esteem of its seriously mentally ill participants. Aspects of the setting that facilitated access and ongoing participation are examined below.

Description of the Project

The Community Connections Project is staffed by two clinical psychologists and a psychiatric social worker, with consultation from a psychiatrist and an occupational therapist. Based on an initial professional psychosocial assessment, the client and the professional agree on an individually tailored plan based on the client's special needs and strengths.

Clients with DSM-III-R Axis I or Axis II diagnoses are eligible for services (American Psychological Association, 1987). Because of other services in the area for the demented individual or the practicing alcoholic, these individuals are referred elsewhere. The only other restriction is for persons who can be considered to pose a risk of violence to others; the emphasis on mixing mentally ill and healthy participants does not provide for adequate security measures to work with violent clients.

The range of services includes psychiatric assessment and follow-up, individual and group counseling (by professionals, paraprofessionals, and interns), socialization (rehabilitative day care), care coordination (case management by professionals and volunteers), support groups, "healthy living classes," art therapy, and multiple volunteer opportunities for clients. In-home services are provided through a volunteer "care coordination program" that includes a professional assessment prior to volunteer assignments.

Professional intervention is used only as needed (for example, during periods of decompensation, for particularly complicated case management situations, for interagency "doctor-to-doctor" discussions). Seldom is a "therapist" the only source of support; a sense of community and of empowerment is created by fostering multiple supports and making new roles available to clients. Other nontraditional components include the very nature of the setting as described, the pairing of age-peer paraprofessionals with seriously mentally ill clients whenever appropriate, client volunteerism, a health education emphasis composed of classes and workshops open to the older adult public, and an organizational push toward empowerment and advocacy.

Innovative Program Components

The program includes several innovative components.

Peer Counseling. Senior Health and Peer Counseling began peer counseling services in 1978, initially using trainers from the University of Southern California's Andrus Gerontology Center and other specialists in the field. As new groups of fifteen to twenty-five trainees were trained annually, Senior Health and Peer Counseling developed a specialized training program that was outlined in a manual—*Peer Counseling for Seniors: A Trainer's Guide*—published in 1986. Training efforts have expanded beyond the organization's volunteers. After being featured on *60 Minutes* in 1984, the model was replicated beyond Southern California. Trainings have resulted in the adaptation of the model in several states, and consultation with organizations have taken place in a variety of regions. The manual has been translated into Spanish and Danish, and it is being used to replicate programs across the country. In 1988, the National Institute of Mental Health, through a three-year grant administered by the California State Department of Mental Health, funded the organization to conduct training for peer counseling throughout the state. This project has prepared people at thirty-nine sites to train peer counseling volunteers.

The growing use of peer counseling is easily understood, because it is *affordable* and *acceptable* to older adults, and several studies have now been published that support the need for and value of these programs in a variety of settings (Hoffman, 1983; Losee, Aurebach, and Parham, 1988; Redburn and Juretich, 1989; Scharlach, 1988).

The use of peer counselors with seriously mentally ill clients has not been documented in the literature. Experiences at Senior Health and Peer Counseling demonstrate that, with proper support, peer counselors can be trained to work effectively with clients of this population once the clients have progressed from acute to more stable phases of their illnesses. From the outset of the Community Connections Project, peer counseling has been viewed as an invaluable resource along the continuum of services offered to seriously mentally ill clients.

Volunteerism. In keeping with its mission, Senior Health and Peer Counseling utilizes over 300 volunteers in a variety of roles. The literature highlights the beneficial effects to older adults of affiliation, social ties, and reciprocity (see Antonucci and Akiyama, 1991). Volunteers are honored for their work through recognition luncheons and the marking of special occasions, such as birthdays. Celebrations for staff and for volunteers as well as support during periods of loss are part and parcel of the organization and contribute to the sense of community. A monthly newsletter highlights volunteers, and it is with a great sense of pride that

Community Connections volunteers tell their stories. This is frequently the first time these clients have ever received any kind of positive recognition.

Volunteerism on the part of clients is an explicit objective of the Community Connections Project. Volunteerism provides affiliation, as well as the experience of productivity associated with "aging well" (Herzog and House, 1991). Volunteer projects are identified that provide opportunities for altruism and personal gratification leading to enhanced self-esteem. Included are an ongoing weekly crafts workshop, in which products are designed to benefit other groups such as children in the hospital, nursing home residents, and homebound elderly. Intergenerational projects are planned, the most long-standing being a *Grandfriends Program,* which has expanded to place volunteers at three nursery school sites. It is important to note that these projects are open to all volunteers, which results in a mix of relatively healthy adults and chronically mentally ill.

Health Education. A grant from the U.S. Department of Education has expanded this component of service; Senior Health and Peer Counseling and the Santa Monica Emeritus College offer ten "Healthy Living" classes targeted for older adults having, or at risk of having, serious mental illness. At least 50 percent of each class is "at risk." The classes are generally taught by mental health staff and often include special support groups facilitated by peer counselors. Instructors and support group leaders become important components of the client's expanding support network and treatment team. Examples of class subjects are memory, nutrition, depression, myths of aging, volunteering in one's community, one's unfinished past, and journal writing. The students' ratings of life satisfaction are monitored throughout their participation in the program.

Advocacy. Senior Health and Peer Counseling is committed to advocacy for the needs of older adults. The peer counseling model is in itself an important advocacy tool and has drawn national attention to the emotional needs of older adults over the past seven years through television programs such as *60 Minutes* and *20/20.*

The organization's leadership is active on local and state committees, in networking with other organizations, and in training of students from multiple disciplines. These efforts serve to inform the general public and the professional community as to the need for, and immense value of, services addressing the health and welfare of older adults.

Within the organization, clients' ideas are encouraged through their involvement on internal advisory committees. Clients are informed of and encouraged to participate in the organization's broader advocacy efforts through orientation-group discussions and through our monthly client newsletter. The emphasis is on self-help and on what can be done as a prescription for empowerment of older adults.

Constant threats of cutbacks of funding within Los Angeles county have frequently served as a mechanism to empower clients to take an active role in advocating for the continuation of services that benefit their lives. A recent funding crisis resulted in strengthening the organization's sense of community.

Case Studies

Two case studies will help to give the preceding discussion a more concrete dimension.

Margaret was referred by another agency three years ago. At the time, she expressed feeling abandoned and was extremely suspicious and frightened about starting treatment. She lived alone and had unstable family support, no friends, and an extensive psychiatric history including several hospitalizations. Margaret was gradually introduced to services, beginning with weekly counseling sessions by a staff person. Extremely sensitive, she at first regretted her growing self-disclosure in sessions and called the therapist to express paranoid distortions about the sessions or to ask for demonstrations of caring. After several months, and two near hospitalizations, she agreed to see the agency's consulting psychiatrist for medication consultation. A medication was identified that greatly improved her paranoia and impulse control. Although her compliance waxed and waned, she was responsive to requests that she resume medication. Once relatively stable, she was eager to try other services and was introduced to a crafts workshop, where her sense of attachment and industry grew. She offered her services during center celebrations and became recognized for her hand-crafted centerpieces. Her growth extended to the greater community, where she joined a weight loss group, made some enduring friends, and won the state competition for weight loss last year. She also began to attend "Healthy Living" classes, which have given her an increasing comfort with peers. Although still vulnerable to stress, the client recaptures her strengths more quickly than in the past. She maintains a sense of integrity and connectedness to others that she reports as a new experience.

David was trained six years ago in the peer counseling program, but he has not seen peer counseling clients for several years due to periodic battles with major depression. A Christian Scientist, he has declined medication despite the serious symptoms of his recurrent disorder. Instead, he seeks emotional support from another peer counselor and maintains his sense of purpose by pursuing two less demanding volunteer tasks at the agency—friendly visiting and phone work in the intake office. A retired teacher, he maintains interest in continuing education, and he is a frequent enrollee in the "Healthy Living" classes. David's peer counselor for four years has seen him through depressive episodes, continually reassuring him that they will pass, as indeed they do. When he has had suicidal ideation, he and the peer counselor receive extra support from agency professional staff; when free of symptoms, he and his counselor cut back their sessions to once a month, with phone support as needed. David's values and sense of self are preserved through the service modes offered him.

Suggestions for Action

Our experience in consulting with other agencies with different demographics and needs tells us that the basic programmatic concepts presented in this chapter can be adapted to a variety of settings, such as hospitals, religious organizations, community mental health clinics, and any number of residential settings. The key elements to be incorporated are the pairing of professionals and paraprofessionals, flexibility to adapt services to client's changing needs, and opportunities for developing of strengths and a sense of community, such as client participation in student, volunteer, and advocacy roles.

Funding for mental health services to older adults is difficult to obtain, and for a nontraditional approach it is almost impossible to find. Senior Health and Peer Counseling could not have initiated the Community Connections Project without the willingness of the Robert Wood Johnson Foundation to support a unique project. Likewise, it could not be sustained without a diversified funding base consisting of extensive fundraising activities, public support directed primarily at case management and socialization, and some Medicare reimbursement. Other critical grants were obtained from the U.S. Department of Education for "Healthy Living" classes and from foundation support, which assisted in initiating Medicare billing. Indeed, attention to grant development of opportunities and private sector fundraising have been crucial to the continuation of the project.

The Community Connections Project furnishes an excellent example of an innovative approach for providing a continuum of mental health services to older adults that empowers and encourages participants to become involved with their communities. Utilizing older adults in paraprofessional volunteer roles makes the program cost effective and expandable. It establishes a system of care adaptable to clients' needs, resulting in high service utilization and low attrition. It is clear that the intervention incorporated reduces the incidence of hospitalizations, homelessness, and desperate acts, while improving clients' sense of integrity within a community. Community Connections is an approach that overcomes the barriers to mental health services for older adults.

References

Acosta, S. T., Cohen, D., Green, C., and Wulke, H. "California Senior Legislature Proposal for Older Adults Mental Health Act." Unpublished proposal, California Senior Legislature, Sacramento, 1991.

American Psychological Association. *Diagnostic and Statistical Manual of Mental Disorders.* (3rd ed.) Washington, D.C.: American Psychological Association, 1987.

Antonucci, T., and Akiyama, H. "Social Relationships and Aging Well: How Do They Exert Their Salubrious Effects?" *Generations,* 1991, *15* (1), 39–44.

Atchley, R. C. *Social Forces and Aging: An Introduction to Social Gerontology.* (4th ed.) Belmont, Calif.: Wadsworth, 1985.

Butler, R., and Lewis, M. *Aging and Mental Health.* St. Louis, Mo.: Mosby, 1982.

Chambre, S. M. *Good Deeds in Old Age: Volunteering by the New Leisure Class.* Lexington, Mass.: Lexington Books, 1987.

Curian, B. "Mental Health Outreach and Consultation Services for the Elderly." *Hospital and Community Psychiatry,* 1982, *33* (2), 142–147.

Herzog, A. R., and House, J. S. "Productive Activities and Aging Well: Meaningful but Flexible Opportunities Are Needed." *Generations,* 1991, *15* (1), 49–54.

Hoffman, S. B. "Peer Counseling Training with the Elderly." *Gerontologist,* 1983, *23,* 358–360.

Kramer, M., Tauge, C., and Redick, R. "Patterns of Use of Psychiatric Facilities by the Aged: Past, Present, and Future." In C. Eisdorfer and M. P. Lawton (eds.), *The Psychology of Adult Development and Aging.* Washington, D.C.: American Psychological Association, 1973.

Losee, N., Auerbach, S. M., and Parham, I. "Effectiveness of a Peer Counselor Hotline for the Elderly." *Journal of Community Psychology,* 1988, *16,* 428–436.

Melcher, J. "Keeping Our Elderly Out of Institutions by Putting Them Back in Their Homes." *American Psychologist,* 1988, *43* (8), 643–647.

Pfeiffer, E. "Psychopathology and Social Psychology." In J. E. Birren and K. W. Schaie (eds.), *Handbook of the Psychology of Aging.* New York: Van Nostrand Reinhold, 1977.

Redburn, D. E., and Juretich, M. "Some Considerations for Using Widowed Self-Help Group Leaders." *Gerontology and Geriatrics Education,* 1989, *9* (3), 89–98.

Ross, M. (ed.). *Peer Counseling for Seniors: A Trainer's Guide.* Santa Monica, Calif.: Senior Health and Peer Counseling, 1986.

Scharlach, A. "Peer Counselor Training for Nursing Home Residents." *Gerontologist,* 1988, *28* (4), 499–502.

Srole, L., Langer, T. S., Michael, S. T., Opler, M. K., and Renne, T.A.C. *Mental Health in the Metropolis: The Midtown Manhattan Study.* New York: McGraw-Hill, 1962.

Whelihan, W. M. "Traditional Modalities Can Work for Older People Too." *Generations,* 1979, *3* (4), 18–19.

Zarit, S. H. *Aging and Mental Disorders.* New York: Free Press, 1980.

MARLA HASSINGER MARTIN, *director of mental health services at Senior Health and Peer Counseling, is a geropsychologist and maintains a clinical staff appointment at the UCLA Neuropsychiatric Institute.*

BERNICE BRATTER, *a licensed marriage and family therapist, is the executive director of Senior Health and Peer Counseling and pursues advocacy efforts on behalf of older adults through local and state participation.*

In most states, we reneged on our promise to provide community-based program support to persons deinstitutionalized from psychiatric hospitals. Now many people are blaming those with mental illness for their failure to thrive and have begun creating new laws and methods for reinstitutionalization. This chapter describes a community-based program that is demonstrably effective. It involves the full participation of homeless people diagnosed with mental illness and attests to what can work.

LAMP in L.A.'s Skid Row: A Model for Community-Based Support Services

Mollie Lowery

Many people have asked me to tell the story of Los Angeles Men's Place (LAMP)—how we got started, what some of the struggles have been along the way, and how we have collectively managed to become a creative, effective model for serving the needs of homeless individuals diagnosed with serious mental illness. When people ask how to duplicate LAMP in their own cities, they are most often looking for short-order recipes that can be microwaved rather than baked in a slow oven. It takes time to build community! The essence of LAMP *is* community, as well as process—a dynamic, inclusive, responsive process. What we have done *can* be duplicated . . . with vision, time, and commitment.

Description of LAMP Programs and Development

In June 1985, we opened the doors of our LAMP Drop-In Center. We founded LAMP on the following principles: services would be completely voluntary and accessible; agency growth and administration would be driven by the needs of the people served; staff would represent the diversity of the population served and would therefore include people diagnosed with mental illness; "guests" (program participants) would have the opportunity to work for and with the agency as it grew; we would be a lifelong, nonlinear service network providing a continuum of support; and we would grow into a community working toward constructive, individual, collective, and systemic change.

Located in the heart of Skid Row, LAMP Drop-In Center is open seven days a week and meets basic survival needs for food, clothing, hot showers, and toilets. We also provide health screening, a mailing address, services as "payee" for Social Security benefits; and advocacy services for housing, entitlements, and legal problems. LAMP is a safe place—a clean, caring, reliable, respectful home base. Our focus is on bringing people in off the streets, building trust, and establishing a healthy, accepting, dependable community of staff and guests.

Within our first four months of operation, we were seeing more than eighty people each day—people diagnosed with schizophrenia and bipolar disorder; people who had been avoiding contact with any traditional programs or services and who had, up to that point, found barely surviving on the streets the only tolerable alternative. They came to LAMP because we provide them with the space, time, and resources to determine for themselves what their needs are and when and how to meet those needs.

The persons we had difficulty with included those who had a primary diagnosis of addiction, those with an extensive history of violence, and those diagnosed as "sociopathic." Since most of these individuals use manipulation, deceit, and criminal behavior to survive, it is difficult to change this behavior in LAMP's loosely structured environment. In continuing to work with these people, we screen carefully and set specific, clear limits and consequences in the beginning.

In our first year of operation, we forged an effective relationship with the County Skid Row Mental Health Clinic, two blocks away from LAMP. As our guests' basic survival needs were met, and they built friendships at LAMP and developed an increased sense of self-worth, they could consider their longer-range physical and mental health needs and pursue them. They could set some priorities and had the self-confidence to explore and choose an acceptable level of psychiatric "treatment." The County Clinic continued modifying its structure to accommodate street people, allowing drop-in clients, discussing medications or dosages with their patients, and doing some street and downtown hotel outreach. They became a more effective resource, and the partnership between LAMP and Skid Row Mental Health has made more comprehensive care possible, accessible, and affordable.

Meanwhile, back at LAMP Drop-In Center, as our population grew, an overnight encampment took root in front of the building. Up to twenty LAMP guests were sleeping next to LAMP rather than in the local mission beds. Guests insisted that it was safer and friendlier to sleep on LAMP's parking lot and sidewalk. In response, in March 1987, we began providing crisis shelter services, housing eighteen guests each night in our Drop-in Center building. In the tradition already established by the LAMP Drop-in Center, there was no time limit set for shelter stay. People were welcome to stay as long as they met our criteria and followed some basic rules. The rules at LAMP were simple and straightforward: no violence, including destruction or theft of property; no threats of violence; come in reasonably sober.

During our first two years of operation, we pushed sobriety and banned the obvious addicts. It became clear that 50 to 60 percent of the guests had, in addition to their mental illness, serious problems with drugs and alcohol. We had to take their unmet needs seriously. Our first attempt to confront the drug abuse problems among guests was to try to utilize existing drug recovery and treatment programs through referral. The two-month waiting periods, required daily phone contacts, and limited beds for each category of drug or alcohol dependence were standard frustrations. The greatest barrier was the traditional program ban against use of any psychotropic medications. As we attempted to refer our guests, it became more apparent that the drug treatment programs were not accessible to our "dual-diagnosed" guests. We began working on our own in-house drug recovery program.

Our staff took several months to educate ourselves, work with outside trainers, and change old attitudes that interfered with our ability to work effectively with addicted persons. Our dual-diagnosed guests were difficult to work with. (Most of our staff felt they should just sober up and quit being obnoxious.) LAMP gradually hired some recovering staff, including previous LAMP guests. Drug recovery became a special focus integrated into all our programs. Added funding to support the drug recovery component came from County Mental Health.

As our LAMP community evolved, continuing to include new people, different needs emerged. Guests wanted more program options and resources to continue their growth. Most of them identified employment as a natural next step, especially when they saw some of their friends become LAMP staff. In response to these rising expectations, we discussed plans for developing a transitional residence and some type of small, income-generating business.

Because LAMP now had a proven track record, in 1987 we were approached by a few community leaders who had been meeting with city and county officials concerning the use of a city warehouse/garage in Skid Row and $1,000,000 in county monies that were earmarked for the homeless. They asked if LAMP could use the site and the funds. The answer was a resounding yes, and LAMP Village Transitional Residence and our small businesses were in the making.

After one full year of delays due to the local businesspeople's opposition to our zoning variance, in late 1988 we were able to begin construction on the 30,000-square-foot brick warehouse. Under the one roof, LAMP Village would house a forty-eight-bed transitional residence with a full program of life-skills workshops; performance, visual art, and writing classes; and drug recovery, case management, and advocacy services. It would also include four businesses providing jobs for LAMP guests and some basic community amenities in the Skid Row area: a commercial linen service, a laundromat, a minimarket, and public showers and toilets.

By 1988–1989, the LAMP community was demonstrating some additional successes. Our staff of fifteen included a cook and two staff advocates who were "graduates" of LAMP. This had been a goal, but achieving it took sustained, focused effort. Staff with university education and degrees had to wrestle with their own biases because life experience was valued equally to traditional education. Our guest "graduates" had to make the complex, sometimes agonizing transition from being LAMP guests to being full-time, paid staff. Usually this involved a change in residence, letting go of some less stable friends and social connections, and earning a salary instead of collecting Social Security and Medi-Cal benefits. This transition took time, trial and error, and genuine support from other LAMP staff. One necessity most difficult to obtain was health coverage that could accommodate reasonable psychiatric care. To augment services not paid for by insurance, LAMP built an expanded "in-house support system"—allowing for flexible shift scheduling and providing a counselor (at no cost to staff) to do group and individual counseling.

In response to Skid Row need and increasing numbers of women showing up on our doorstep, LAMP began serving women as well as men. And, I believe, LAMP was reducing the need for hospitalizations. Whereas in the first two years at least a dozen LAMP guests were hospitalized one or more times, by 1989 only three guests became so dysfunctional that they needed acute hospitalization. The consistency and reliability of the LAMP community give our guests an anchor to hold onto as they cycle through mental illness. Our guests began relying more and more on each other for help, as friends and family.

During the early stages of the Village development, we experimented with permanent housing. Believing that LAMP guests would want to move out of the area and off Skid Row, we quietly leased a small apartment building in Santa Monica and began moving guests in. A staff person lived in one of the units, mostly to provide support. The distance between LAMP Drop-In Center/Shelter and the apartments was fifteen miles. In Los Angeles, that translates into a one-hour bus ride. For eighteen months, the housing experiment stumbled along half full most of the time. Only one guest actually acclimated successfully to the new setting. Everyone else returned to LAMP on Skid Row. Guests said repeatedly that the apartments were just too far from "home." They felt alienated and isolated away from their friends and family at LAMP. This experience was crucial, because it determined the direction of LAMP's future development. Rather than relate to Skid Row as an undesirable, temporary situation to escape from, we would turn our energies to investing in and improving the area in an effort to make it a better, more decent, livable residential neighborhood.

In the spring of 1990, representatives of the Community Redevelopment Agency offered LAMP a fifty-two-unit single-room occupancy (SRO) building located in Skid Row. The building was in the midst of major renovation when the former owner ceased operating and abandoned the project. It is within walking distance from LAMP Drop-In Center/Shelter and LAMP Village. We took the CRA offer, and in June 1990, LAMP began construction on our new permanent housing, LAMP Lodge. In the same month, LAMP Village went into operation.

Our LAMP Village building is one city block long and 200 feet wide, with 30-foot ceilings and lots of natural light and space. It houses two distinct operations—a transitional residence and four small businesses.

The residential program is goal oriented, focused on development of the "whole" person and on preparing individuals for more independent living. In the beginning, the emphasis was on in-house group work and classes. We gradually modified this and have tailored our services more to the guests' individual needs and goals. We also utilize some resources outside of the Village—the YMCA, Skid Row Mental Health Socialization, and AA/NA meetings. Our on-site performing/visual/writing arts classes have been highly successful in bringing out the creative, emotional, and artistic side of our guests. "Operation Hammer," a performance troupe, has done shows developed from their own material at Equity-waiver theaters in Los Angeles. LAMP guests who have moved into the Village and committed themselves to participating in the full program for several months have made significant life changes through the process. Their mental illness remains but does not dominate or drive their day-to-day choices. Self-confidence and reliance have replaced self-hate and dependence. They look to the months ahead, not just to tomorrow, with hope and plans. For many of the guests, a significant factor in this change has been the opportunity for employment in the Village businesses.

One half of the LAMP Village facility houses four small businesses, three of which went into operation in the fall of 1990, subsidized by a five-year grant from the Robert Wood Johnson Foundation. The combination of businesses is designed to provide a variety of job experiences and levels of responsibility and skill. In addition, they are an investment in, contribution to, and resource for the residents of Skid Row.

The Village Linen Service contracts with nonprofit hotel, shelter, and recovery home operators. The service cleans and delivers linens, towels, and blankets at commercially competitive prices, promising quality work professionally delivered and a role in employing people who have been homeless and are diagnosed with mental illness. As of summer 1991, the Village Linen Service employed fifteen LAMP guests part time and had 60 percent of the contracts needed to break even financially.

Our LAMP Village Laundromat is the only self-service coin-op laundry in the forty square blocks called Skid Row. Since our opening, we have been operating at maximum capacity. Plans are underway to begin a "fluff and fold" operation to generate additional income and to utilize more guest-employees.

The Village Public Toilets and Showers, known fondly as the Village "PiTS," make a real contribution to the quality of life for Skid Row inhabitants. Hot showers with towels and soap cost 25 cents for five minutes; use of the toilets is free. Staffing these facilities requires the employment of up to three guest-employees, whose duties include supervision, dispensing towels, and maintenance. There are no other public bathrooms or showers available on Skid Row.

Our fourth business, soon to open, is the Village Market—a clean, honest, reasonably priced source of daily necessities, food items, toiletries, and paper products. It will be an alternative to the existing numerous liquor stores that sell cheap fortified wines, crack paraphernalia, and overpriced food items.

Our guest-employees in the Village Businesses work part time, earning minimum wage, and continue to draw Social Security benefits. One of our goals is to eventually move people into full-time work, increased pay, and off SSI. To achieve this, the businesses themselves must mature and the guest-employees need to feel confident that the jobs are there and that they, individually, have the capacity to sustain employment. To that end, all guest-employees participate in a weekly support group with a counselor. The guest-employees are paid for this time. They also have the option of doing individual sessions with the counselor, on their own time. Most guest-employees look forward to the group, and many request individual time.

In July 1991, our LAMP Lodge construction was completed and the units were ready for occupancy. LAMP now has fifty apartments—permanent, affordable, and fully furnished, with a private bathroom and kitchen in each. Within five blocks of LAMP Day Center and LAMP Village, the LAMP Lodge completes a continuum of housing and support services. In the now well-established tradition of LAMP, two "graduates" of our guest population were hired into full-time positions at the Lodge—the live-in manager and the maintenance person. A few guest-tenants are employed part time as desk clerks. After the first fifteen people moved in, a Tenant Council was established allowing tenants to increase their direct participation in decisions and policy-making at the Lodge.

Strengths of the LAMP Program

Eight strengths should be highlighted.

Nonlinear and Lifelong Orientation. We have no cures for schizophrenia and bipolar disorder. Most survivors of these chronic illnesses experience their first symptoms as teenagers or young adults. Many will live their entire lives struggling and coping with them. With or without medication, they will experience acute cycles. LAMP programs are developed on the assumption that our guests need lifelong support and treatment. Our service and housing components are nonlinear in that guests can utilize whatever services or level of housing they need or can function in now, and repeatedly. Guests do not need to move from A to B to C. They do not fail or graduate from the LAMP community. They grow, learn, and change. And, yes, they question and refuse medications periodically, experiment with drugs and sex, travel impulsively in hopes their schizophrenic symptoms will change with the new environment, and spend all of their SSI money on a junk car that gets impounded the first day. And LAMP is still there, to grow in, to fall apart in, to come back to, to stay at . . . no time limit on healing. Because the LAMP community is there through it all, they have a secure, safe place and constructive relationships so they can continue learning from these experiences. There is nothing unique in this concept. This is how we all learn and have the support to change our lives.

Emphasis on Community. Once a person is screened into LAMP, he or she is a part of the lifelong community. It has taken time and focused effort to build an inclusive, strong community among guests and staff. We want a community that thrives in and respects its diversity of race, ethnicity, class, sexual orientation or preference, level of education, and life experience. From our beginnings, the LAMP staff has been representative of the guest population with regard to race, ethnicity, class, and sexuality. Within eighteen months of operation, we were able to bring guests onto the staff. As of 1991, 38 percent of the forty-five LAMP staff are former or current guests. This staff integration and the growth of LAMP services have resulted in a solid, resourceful community that provides for growth and change. This community is a process for us—a constant challenge to our attitudes concerning power, ownership, and control and a struggle against the internalized, societally reinforced assumption that people with mental illness are "in-valids," unwilling or unable to control their own lives.

Importance of Change Rather Than Adjustment. We work for change—constructive, individual, collective, and systemic change. We are not invested in assisting people to adjust better to a defined status quo. We want our guests to discover their own purpose, to be active in creating their individual destinies. As LAMP community members, we work together to be a part of the solution to societal and systemic problems.

Voluntary Nature. Every element of LAMP's programs is completely voluntary. People choose from the range of services, what they are ready for and when. This includes use of psychotropic medications, level of housing, and participation in drug recovery. The staff and the larger LAMP community are there to facilitate constructive decisions and change. Every day, we prove that if people diagnosed with serious mental illness are provided with safe, accessible, respectful services, they *will* use them. Most of our guests have avoided systems of care because they have been coerced into treatment. Like most people, they want to understand and have some control over their own health treatment. They have legitimate questions and concerns about the medications. We find that if we take the time to give them the information, good and bad, many of them do choose the medications rather than no treatment at all.

Safety and Accessibility. LAMP feels safe because our community acts as its own security system. We work together to maintain a nonviolent environment. For those who first come to LAMP, this can be difficult. Their life on the streets has required aggression to survive. They learn quickly that at LAMP, this violence is unnecessary and unacceptable. Their survival needs are provided for without their having to yell, bang on doors, "act crazy," or wait for hours. Their time and needs are respected and responded to with consistency and dignity. Staff are pivotal in providing a sense of safety. As staff, we must have our own issues of control and aggression worked out. We have to know when it is important to limit a guest's actions or discipline a guest, and when it is better to back away to avoid exacerbating violence. The LAMP rules are few and basic, easy to remember, and clear.

LAMP is accessible—physically, emotionally, and spiritually. Our buildings have ample space for the numbers of people we serve. We all participate in keeping the buildings in good repair and clean. We minimize the numbers of areas or rooms that must be locked and off limits to certain people. Our buildings are designed to use lots of natural light. We decorate with guest and staff art. As a community, we work at building tolerance and respect for each other. It matters that people feel safe and free to express constructive anger, joy, excitement, and creativity. So many of our guests, as people with mental illness, have learned that such expressions are wrong.

Demystification of Mental Illness and More. At LAMP, we make every effort to talk about mental illness with the same frequency, intensity, and casualness as sex, drugs, news, food, money, movies, and politics. For those people in our LAMP community who must live with it all their lives, half the battle is accepting mental illness as part of themselves and not some alien experience to be dreaded and struggled against.

We talk about drugs a lot because many people in the LAMP community use them, prescribed or not. Society sees some of the drugs as good and important to take (psychotropic medication) and some as immoral and bad for everyone (heroin, cocaine, and so on). Regardless of our own individual beliefs and values, many persons with mental illness are going to question and challenge the assumptions that one drug is better than another for making them feel better. The fact is, most of the dual-diagnosed individuals that LAMP works with take crack initially because it feels better than prolixin or haldol. If we accept this as a reality, acknowledge the benefits and negatives of both prescribed drugs and street drugs, consider the greater availability of street drugs over pre-scribed medications, and provide a lifelong, strong, supportive commu-nity, an individual stands a much better chance of choosing sobriety.

Guest Employment. We employ LAMP guests because we seek work as an important opportunity for individuals to grow, build confidence in themselves, and take pride in their lives. We employ LAMP guests because there is a lot of work to be done, and some of them can do it better than anyone else. Finally, we employ guests because it is a defini-tive way to build an inclusive community of people who are invested in their own individual life goals as well as the collective goals of the LAMP community.

It works because we have created a diversity of *real* jobs and built in a consistent, supportive work environment; we pay guests fairly and protect their rights as employees through personnel policies; and they have opportunities for advancement. (Former and current LAMP guests are in positions that earn anywhere from $4.25 an hour to $28,000 a year plus benefits.) The weekly support group provides a sounding board and a place to discuss personal and work-related problems. Every payday, another group forms to discuss the stresses and decisions about the use of the hard-earned money. The group usually focuses on the need for everyone to come to work the next day regardless of whether they partied all night.

LAMP Administrative Structure. To effectively implement the goals and philosophy of the LAMP programs, we have worked hard to maintain an administrative structure that can provide the flexibility, accountabil-ity, and leadership necessary. It allows for maximum participation of all staff in direct service and minimizes the differentiation between adminis-trative and line staff and guests. Shared decision making is built in. All staff (bookkeeper, janitor, cook, program directors, and so on) are in-volved in trainings and with program evaluation and planning. Interper-sonal communication is encouraged and used more than dependence on written memos and procedures. All staff are informed about agency funding and its sources. We make conscious decisions about what mon-ies to accept or reject based on our collective understanding of LAMP's goals and purpose. How we work together as staff must be a model for and encourage the building of community.

A Final Note on Replication

All of what we have done is possible in any and every neighborhood. The key ingredients are vision, respect, common sense, passion, clarity of goals, understanding, and commitment; some savvy about how to raise money; fearlessness in the face of prejudice and ignorance; and time, patience, and the courage to learn and change with experience. These are the elements of long-term solutions. We can make the time, generate the will, and create the resources. The health, growth, and quality of people's lives, of our communities, depend on our collective good use of them.

MOLLIE LOWERY is founding executive director of LAMP, Inc., in Los Angeles, and she has worked with the homeless mentally ill since 1975.

INDEX

ORDERING INFORMATION

NEW DIRECTIONS FOR MENTAL HEALTH SERVICES is a series of paperback books that presents timely and readable volumes on subjects of concern to clinicians, administrators, and others involved in the care of the mentally disabled. Each volume is devoted to one topic and includes a broad range of authoritative articles written by noted specialists in the field. Books in the series are published quarterly in fall, winter, spring, and summer and are available for purchase by subscription as well as by single copy.

SUBSCRIPTIONS for 1992 cost $52.00 for individuals (a savings of 20 percent over single-copy prices) and $70.00 for institutions, agencies, and libraries. Please do not send institutional checks for personal subscriptions. Standing orders are accepted.

SINGLE COPIES cost $17.95 when payment accompanies order. (California, New Jersey, New York, and Washington, D.C., residents please include appropriate sales tax.) Billed orders will be charged postage and handling.

DISCOUNTS for quantity orders are available. Please write to the address below for information.

ALL ORDERS must include either the name of an individual or an official purchase order number. Please submit your order as follows:
  Subscriptions: specify series and year subscription is to begin
  Single copies: include individual title code (such as MHS1)

Mail all orders to:
  Jossey-Bass Publishers
  350 Sansome Street
  San Francisco, California 94104

For sales outside of the United States contact:
  Maxwell Macmillan International Publishing Group
  866 Third Avenue
  New York, New York 10022

OTHER TITLES AVAILABLE IN THE
NEW DIRECTIONS FOR MENTAL HEALTH SERVICES SERIES
H. RICHARD LAMB, EDITOR-IN-CHIEF

U.S. Postal Service
STATEMENT OF OWNERSHIP, MANAGEMENT AND CIRCULATION
Required by 39 U.S.C. 3685

1A. Title of Publication	1B. PUBLICATION NO.									2. Date of Filing
NEW DIRECTIONS FOR MENTAL HEALTH SERVICES	4	9	3	–	9	1	0			10/16/92

3. Frequency of Issue	3A. No. of Issues Published Annually	3B. Annual Subscription Price
Quarterly	Four (4)	$52(individual) $70(institutional)

4. Complete Mailing Address of Known Office of Publication (Street, City, County, State and ZIP + 4 Code) (Not printers)

350 Sansome Street, San Francisco, CA 94104-1310

5. Complete Mailing Address of the Headquarters of General Business Offices of the Publisher (Not printer)

(above address)

6. Full Names and Complete Mailing Address of Publisher, Editor, and Managing Editor (This item MUST NOT be blank)
Publisher (Name and Complete Mailing Address)

Jossey-Bass Inc., Publishers (see address at 4.)

Editor (Name and Complete Mailing Address)

H. Richard Lamb, Department of Psychiatry and Behavioral Sciences, U.S.C.
School of Medicine, 1934 Hospital Place, Los Angeles, CA 90033

Managing Editor (Name and Complete Mailing Address)

Lynn Luckow, President, Jossey-Bass Inc., Publishers (see address at 4.)

7. Owner (If owned by a corporation, its name and address must be stated and also immediately thereafter the names and addresses of stockholders owning or holding 1 percent or more of total amount of stock. If not owned by a corporation, the names and addresses of the individual owners must be given. If owned by a partnership or other unincorporated firm, its name and address, as well as that of each individual must be given. If the publication is published by a nonprofit organization, its name and address must be stated.) (Item must be completed.)

Full Name	Complete Mailing Address
Maxwell Communications Corp., plc	Headington Hill Hall Oxford OX30BW U.K.

8. Known Bondholders, Mortgagees, and Other Security Holders Owning or Holding 1 Percent or More of Total Amount of Bonds, Mortgages or Other Securities (If there are none, so state)

Full Name	Complete Mailing Address
same address as 7.	same address as 7.

9. For Completion by Nonprofit Organizations Authorized To Mail at Special Rates (DMM Section 423.12 only)
The purpose, function, and nonprofit status of this organization and the exempt status for Federal income tax purposes (Check one)

☐ (1) Has Not Changed During Preceding 12 Months ☐ (2) Has Changed During Preceding 12 Months *(If changed, publisher must submit explanation of change with this statement.)*

10. Extent and Nature of Circulation (See instructions on reverse side)	Average No. Copies Each Issue During Preceding 12 Months	Actual No. Copies of Single Issue Published Nearest to Filing Date
A. Total No. Copies (Net Press Run)	2000	2076
B. Paid and/or Requested Circulation 1. Sales through dealers and carriers, street vendors and counter sales	1061	846
2. Mail Subscription (Paid and/or requested)	460	>20
C. Total Paid and/or Requested Circulation (Sum of 10B1 and 10B2)	1521	1366
D. Free Distribution by Mail, Carrier or Other Means Samples, Complimentary, and Other Free Copies	142	77
E. Total Distribution (Sum of C and D)	1663	1443
F. Copies Not Distributed 1. Office use, left over, unaccounted, spoiled after printing	337	633
2. Return from News Agents	–0–	–0–
G. TOTAL (Sum of E, F1 and 2—should equal net press run shown in A)	2000	2076

11. I certify that the statements made by me above are correct and complete	Signature and Title of Editor, Publisher, Business Manager, or Owner *[signature]* Larry Ishii Vice-President

PS Form 3526, Feb. 1989 *(See instructions on reverse)*